experiences:
THE 7TH ERA OF MARKETING

HOW BUSINESS WILL BE TRANSFORMED IN A NEW ERA OF MARKETING—
LED BY STORYTELLERS AND POWERED BY REMARKABLE,
CONTENT-DRIVEN, CUSTOMER EXPERIENCES

By Robert Rose & Carla Johnson

About Content Marketing Institute
Content Marketing Institute is the leading global content marketing education and training
organization. CMI teaches enterprise brands how to attract and retain customers through
compelling, multi-channel storytelling. CMI's Content Marketing World event, the largest
content marketing-focused event, is held every September, and Content Marketing World
Sydney, every March. CMI also produces the quarterly magazine *Chief Content Officer,* and
provides strategic consulting and content marketing research for some of the best-known brands
in the world. CMI is a 2012, 2013, and 2014 Inc. 500 company.

www.contentmarketinginstitute.com

Interior layout and design by www.PearCreative.ca

ISBN: 978-0-9859576-4-3

Printed in the United States of America.

Praise for *EXPERIENCES: The 7th Era of Marketing*

"Our ability to connect with customers is harder than ever. Carla and Robert show why marketing is no longer 'business as usual,' and it's time that marketing took a broader and more strategic role in leading the charge."
—Kathy Button Bell, Chief Marketing Officer, Emerson

"Digital, social, and mobile technologies have caused significant changes in the ways brands interact and engage with their customers. We now expect consistent and engaging experiences in every aspect of our lives. The world has changed dramatically; most marketing is highly ineffective at reaching consumers. And Carla and Robert have done a tremendous job in laying out the framework for using experiences to drive results for your marketing efforts."
—Michael Brenner, Marketing Thought Leader, Blogger, Keynote Speaker, and Head of Strategy at NewsCred

"Robert and Carla nail the challenge of marketing to a busy, attention-impaired, fragmented audience who has stopped listening, but not living. This is a compelling treatise, call-to-arms, and self-help guide to creating the experiences that make people fall in love with brands over and over again."
—Julie Fleischer, Director of Data, Content, and Media, Kraft Food Group

"Marketers are battling for attention in the midst of the biggest market disruption since the industrial revolution. Robert and Carla show the impact on marketing, and explain marketing's new role at the executive table."
—Dan Pastuszak, Head of Marketing, LinkedIn, Canada

"Articulating and telling the story is one part of the equation. Operationalizing it is another. Carla and Robert show marketers why they need to understand how to create a framework that lets them take their purpose within the organization—storytelling—and operationalize it across the enterprise."
—Mark Wilson, Senior Vice President, Marketing, BlackBerry

TABLE OF CONTENTS

foreword:
THE MARKETING RENAISSANCE

In the 1300s, Europe experienced an awakening that lasted 300 years. This Renaissance touched everything, from science and literature to art and diplomacy. It was a time when people questioned traditional beliefs and opened their minds to human emotion, intellectual curiosity and cultural experiences. Benchmarks, as we know them, didn't exist; so artists, scientists, and all manner of inventors felt free to explore, experiment, and create value.

Right now, our profession is in the midst of our own awakening.

For decades, marketers have functioned in communication-oriented roles. But now we need a more strategic perspective that reflects the impact that marketing can have on our organizations as a whole. The "Renaissance Marketer" now has the opportunity to work cross-functionally and design the experiences that differentiate. And, as with the Renaissance of the 1300s, there are no benchmarks to measure against.

Right now, marketing as a function is at an inflection point between what we're comfortable with, what we have permission to do, and what's possible. We can't stay married to yesterday and we can't be afraid of tomorrow.

In our changing roles, we have to be purpose-driven, tech-savvy, and experience-centric. We also have to be well-rounded rather than highly specialized. It's time to put structure and relying on old benchmarks aside so that we can find new paths for the work and conversations we must lead. Robert and Carla help us find those paths.

Experiences: The 7th Era of Marketing brings together both the "why" and the "how" of navigating this new landscape. When you think about it, marketing is the only group that touches every department in any organization; we're the common thread that connects everyone. By placing strategy before structure, Robert and Carla show how marketing professionals have to put their purpose—*building audiences and creating differentiating experiences*—at the forefront of everything they do. They also focus on using a repeatable, manageable, and scalable framework to develop a storytelling-focused organization.

Robert and Carla accurately point out how building roles that apply insights from the outside and empowering the people within can create an environment for innovation. This is how marketers will impact the organizations for which they work—by initially captivating employees through the brand's purpose, they will be able to create rich, engaging experiences for their customers.

We have to create interest and awareness in what we sell and stay involved with prospects long after they become customers so that we keep them interested and engaged. And we have to be tech-savvy to master the quality of digital experiences that are now second nature to our customers.

That takes a Renaissance marketer. Robert and Carla can see this shift and understand that there's no such thing as business as usual. Marketers need to relentlessly focus on creating remarkable experiences. They have to turn traditional marketing practices into something distinctive every chance they get.

To be more creative and innovative as marketers, we have to lose our fear of being wrong or failing. We have to break new ground in our roles and embrace the lack of a benchmark to measure against. Armed with a wide set of interests, an avid curiosity, and an aptitude for learning, we need the creative confidence to combine breakthrough ideas with action in a way that improves our companies, our careers, and the experiences we create for customers.

The Renaissance of the 1300s took centuries to transform Europe. The rapid pace of change today is causing us to experience our marketing Renaissance in only decades. It's time that marketers take courage, show up in these critical moments, and create contextually relevant experiences along the way.

Here's to breaking new ground.

Eduardo Conrado
Senior Vice President – Chief Innovation Officer
Motorola Solutions

introduction:
INVENTING THE FUTURE OF MARKETING

"We're not on our journey to save the world but to save ourselves.
But in doing that you save the world. The influence of a vital person
vitalizes." | Joseph Campbell

What do you *really* do?

To be clear, we're not asking that about the business you own or work
for. We'll get to that in due time. Rather, we mean to ask—what do you
really do for a living? If you're reading this book, chances are you serve in
a marketing or communications-related function in your organization.
Your job, in varying degrees, is to communicate the value of the product
or service your company puts in the marketplace, so that more people
might purchase it.

And we have no doubt you do it brilliantly.

You're facing new challenges daily and meeting them. You and your team expertly create unique value propositions. You shine when asked to create marketing strategies that support the features and benefits of the company's product. Your "reasons to believe" are, bar none, almost evangelical in their crisp and focused clarity. Your advertising tactics and conversion metrics are tight. You have wrung every single inefficient process out of the conversion funnel. Every industry best-practice statistic is at your fingertips. And yet, even at the top of your game, today's environment seems more challenging and unwinnable than ever.

Maybe you're finding it increasingly hard to differentiate your product. Perhaps, despite the importance of your work to describe that value, your management team doesn't consider the marketing function a strategic part of the business. Or, even more challenging, maybe the number of new digital channels and platforms that you have to optimize with a limited budget just feels overwhelming. The new expectations of customers feel unfair at times.

Why is marketing being blamed for not "engaging" at every stage of the customer journey—when we don't have the power, budget, or resources to change so many parts of that journey?

Yes, we've been there.

So, what's the challenge? Is it the digital thing? You *know* that the methods customers are using to research, review, purchase, and become loyal to products and services are fundamentally transformed. You can't go to a conference without hearing all about how "digital" is changing the way customers purchase. Yeah, that's not it. You're all over that.

You have a digital strategy. You've deployed a social team, and an e-business team, and a web team, and a mobile initiative. You've got an app!! But it's still not getting any better. We're still not strategic. It's only getting more overwhelming. What's *really* the challenge?

Well, here it is: **It's not just HOW consumers are changing—researching, reviewing, and buying. It's also WHAT THEY VALUE MOST. This is also changing.** And guess what? It's not your product any longer. They value experiences. If you don't offer compelling, differentiated experiences, your current customers will research, look, purchase, and become loyal elsewhere.

DO YOU HAVE A FOMO?

Recent research has shown that young consumers (those under 35) now account for more than $1 trillion of annual consumer spending. As we move into 2015, they are now at the helm of what's being called "the experience economy."[1]

When asked directly, more than 75% of these Millennials said that "when it comes to money, 'experiences' trump 'things'." As Eric Meyerson, head of Consumer Insights at Eventbrite, the company that sponsored the research, said, "We know that engaging in experience helps Millennials form a sense of identity, differently from how other generations defined identity at their same age."

And it's a *fear of missing out* (FOMO) that is driving this sense of identity.

In 2013, the Oxford English dictionary added 65 new words, including "selfie" and "twerk" (yes, really) to our approved lexicon. It also added

FOMO. Research found that 70% of Millennials have this irrational fear—and it's a primary driver for their desire for new experiences.

But it's not only Millennials that are driving this thirst for compelling experiences over products. In another 2013 study of more than 1,000 adults in the U.S. and the U.K., researchers found that in today's "constantly connected" world, people crave sensory experiences over products. In fact, this study found that 81% of Millennials, 79% of Gen Xers, and 78% of Baby Boomers value experiences more than they do material items. Additionally, 64% would rather spend their money on an experience than a product.[2]

Can you imagine then—in the future—perhaps a store where the primary items for sale aren't products or services, but rather "experiences?"

The thing is, it's already here.

THE WORLD'S FIRST EXPERIENCE EMPORIUM

Quick story: March 5th, 1999, was rainy, overcast, one of those cold, spring mornings that gives San Francisco its reputation. But, for Trevor Traina, the weather that day was beautiful. It was an experience he'd never forget.

He was standing on a stage next to the richest man in the world—Bill Gates—who had just bought his company, Compare.Net, for $100 million and was now announcing it to the world. Microsoft was launching a transformative initiative around ecommerce, and Compare. Net was a key piece of it. Gates said: *The Internet has forever changed the way that business is conducted. With these tools, our hope is that the ecommerce opportunity is opened up for everyone."*[3] There's no doubt that it opened up opportunity for Traina.

Compare.Net was the first of what would eventually become five successful companies that Traina would start over the next 15 years. Three others also were sold, including SchemaLogic (sold to Smart Logic), StepUp Commerce (sold to Intuit), and DriverSide.com (sold to Advance Auto Parts). But it may just be the fifth, and latest, that captures the true essence of Traina's passion.

Following the great recession of 2008–2010, Traina recognized that there was a true evolution underway in how consumers looked at the collection of physical goods. As he said to us, *"I observed that the portfolio of physical things available was no longer differentiated or enticing–and that people were really looking to refocus their dollars on more meaningful expenditures."*

Traina's new company is called IfOnly.com. According to Traina, it's the *"world's first emporium for experiences rather than things."* He calls it "IfOnly" because, as he says, "everyone has his own 'if-only.' Your 'if-only' will almost certainly be different than mine—but whatever it is, it can and should be fulfilled."

IfOnly offers highly curated and customized experiences that range from something as simple as a VIP pass and backstage experience at this year's Farm Aid concert to much more intricate adventures such as a two-day trip with acclaimed photographer Russell James to get an "immersive tour" of Jacmel, the artist's enclave on the coast of Haiti.

Each of the experiences on IfOnly.com also supports a charity. For example, if a buyer chooses the two-day trip to Haiti, part of the proceeds goes to benefit the Nomad Two World's Foundation, which supports and promotes artists from indigenous and marginalized communities around the world.

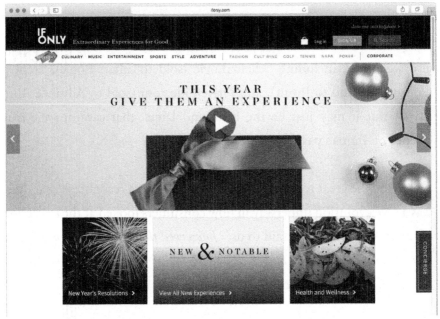

IFOnly.com is the world's first emporium of experiences rather than products. Credit: www.ifonly.com - Screenshot accessed: 11/15/2014

As of the writing of this book, IfOnly is one of the fastest growing companies in San Francisco. It has delivered more than 2,000 experiences in its approximately one year of existence, raised more than $1 million for partner charities, and is adding new global brands, non-profits and customers daily. This rapid growth and interest is a sign, as Traina points out, "*The entire marketing industry is moving to an experience-based economy.*"[4]

SHARE OF EXPERIENCE: THE FUTURE OF MARKETING

At this point you may be asking yourself, "what does Traina's story have to do with my marketing strategy and the question of '**what do I *really* do?**'"

Well, we posed that exact question to Traina. His answer: "*I view IfOnly as a mass-market technology platform. We bring all of the world's top talents in hundreds of different categories—and they can be connected to their natural audiences. I predict all smart brand marketers will begin to re-craft their message into an experiential one. The experiential part of the brand will actually become a secondary source of revenue for the brand.*"

With the success Traina has achieved through the sale of his other companies, we'd all be wise to at least pay attention to this.

And, thus, we go back to our original question.

What do you *really* do? Or rather…what *should you really be doing to prepare for the future?*

Consider a few things.

In a recent (and ongoing) study titled "Marketing2020," Millward Brown Vermeer (previously EffectiveBrands), in concert with the Association of National Advertisers (ANA) and others, asked senior-level marketers to predict what the marketing organization structure will look like in 2020. So far, the study has included in-depth interviews with more than "350 CEOs, CMOs, and agency heads, and more than a dozen CMO roundtables in cities worldwide."[5]

In a July 2014 *Harvard Business Review* article on the study, titled *The Ultimate Marketing Machine*, three contributors to the research—Marc de Swaan Arons, Frank van den Driest, and Keith Weed—conclude (among other things) that to meet this change, marketing organizations must evolve to meet what they call the "total experience." They say:

"Companies are increasingly enhancing the value of their products by creating customer experiences. Some deepen the customer relationship by leveraging what they know about [customers] to personalize offerings. Others focus on the breadth of the relationship by adding touchpoints. Our research shows that high- performing brands do both—providing what we call 'total experience.' In fact, we believe that the most important marketing metric will soon change from 'share of wallet' or 'share of voice' to 'share of experience.'"[6]

We know that content will certainly be at the heart of many, if not most, of these experiences for brands. This is the key. We believe that the new goal of marketing will not be to simply "create a customer." No, the creation of a customer will simply be table stakes for most marketing organizations. The new objective for marketing will be to *evolve a customer*—utilizing differentiating content-driven experiences as the driver of that evolution across the entire lifecycle.

David Edelman and Jason Heller of consulting firm McKinsey identified this as well in October 2014 when they wrote about the disruptions that are driving marketing transformation:

"Continuously evolving customer expectations are a major disruptive force, but marketing is still limited in its ability to shape the entire experience... This lack of responsibility—and accountability—for the entire customer journey will continue to inhibit marketers' efforts to develop seamless and consistent experiences across all touchpoints."[7]

In short, we also believe that marketers must take on new responsibilities and leadership roles. Marketers must not only *describe the value* that has already been theoretically created in the product or service for sale, but also begin to *create differentiated experiential value* that is separate and distinct from that product or service.

MARKETERS CREATE VALUE THROUGH CONTENT-DRIVEN EXPERIENCES

When Traina started Compare.Net in 1996, it was essentially an online comparison-shopping portal. Back then, the Internet was a brand new phenomenon and Traina was excited about how the web could enable brands to turn information about their products from forced advertisement into what he called a "welcome briefing," by simply pairing brands (and their content) with people who were truly looking for a "match."

Ironically, 15 years later, what struck us is that Traina's new business isn't terribly different than the one he started nearly 20 years ago. Today, as he explained to us, his company is talking to "premium automotive brands with very, very expensive vehicles." IfOnly is offering these brands the opportunity to create experiences to test drive high-end cars, visit the factory, and/or consume exclusive content about particular vehicles, reasoning that passionate consumers will happily pay for such experiences. *"These people are, paradoxically, your highest-value prospects, because they are the ones who are most serious about ultimately purchasing,"* Traina says.

And you don't have to look far to see other examples of this cropping up everywhere.

- **Marriott launched a complete original content studio** that will create content-driven experiences in long-form, short form and across all media types. David Beebe, vice president of creative and content marketing, is leading the effort. His background

19

is with Disney-ABC Television Group. He has been quoted as saying that *"while content is just part of the overall travel experience we provide, we believe Marriott can become the world's leading publisher of travel lifestyle content for the next generation."* [8]

- Semiconductor and mobile giant **Qualcomm has created an entire online hub for forward-leaning futurist ideas.** The company created its Qualcomm Spark platform as a way to inspire and ignite conversations about technology. As Liya Sharif, publisher of the platform, said, *"In today's world, consumers are increasingly skeptical of brand messaging and advertising, and the amount of social chatter and noise is deafening. Spark is meant to cut through the noise, reach key audiences with unexpected content and provide a unique perspective from influencers on how mobile is transforming people's lives around the world."* [9]

- **Jyske Bank, one of the largest banks in Denmark, has centered its entire marketing strategy on an Internet-based TV station.** Jyske has transformed into a media company that also happens to sell banking services. Its physical presence now features comfy chairs, magazines, a coffee bar, and a feast of informative and entertaining videos from its 24/7 broadcast offering. [10]

CONTENT IN MARKETING ISN'T NEW, BUT CONTENT MARKETING IS

We often talk about how the use of content-driven experiences for marketing purposes isn't a new practice. For hundreds of years, businesses have been using content in pockets to affect some kind of profitable outcome. But the reality is this: Notwithstanding a few exceptional examples such as John Deere's *The Furrow* from the 1800s, Michelin's travel guides from the early 1900s, and even Hasbro's G.I.

JOE partnership with Marvel in the 1980s, content was not—and is not—a scalable, repeatable practice within the function of marketing. In short, content marketing was historically (and still is almost exclusively) treated as a project, not a process.

That's the part that *has* changed. Whether it's due to the digital disruption and ease by which we now publish and distribute content and experiences to aggregate our own audiences, or just the natural evolution of marketing itself, doesn't matter as much as the ultimate outcome. There can be no argument, as we roll into the next five years and approach 2020, that content—and the exponentially increasing quantities that every organization produces—affects our marketing strategy and should be dealt with as a component of that strategy throughout the enterprise.

Forrester Research predicts that unstructured enterprise content volume is growing at a rate of 200% annually.[11] Enterprises are now functioning as content factories, producing massive mountains of digital files that spew forth from marketing—like a giant Dr. Seuss machine—landing squarely on the back of the content wagon being towed. How much that wagon acts as a differentiator—or as a weight that hinders forward progress—depends on how well the content is managed.

Content *will affect business*—it's just a matter of "how," not "if"—so enterprises must make a choice:

- Content can be managed as the strategic asset that it has (or can) become

- Or, it can be an expensive by-product that ultimately bogs down a company as it tries to navigate the broader disruptions taking place.

EXPERIENCES: THE 7TH ERA OF MARKETING

We contend that we are moving into a new era of marketing. And it's all about experiences that strengthen our customer bonds.

Most marketing textbooks generally agree that marketing as a discipline has evolved over five distinct eras, each lasting about 20 to 30 years.

The first five well-documented eras are the Trade Era, the Production Era, the Sales Era, the Marketing Department Era, and the Marketing Company Era. A sixth era of marketing, the Relationship Era, is generally accepted (though not in most textbooks) as the era we've been operating in for the last 20 years. It started with one-to-one marketing in the mid-1990s, moved into personalization in the early 2000s, and for the last seven years or so has been squarely focused on "engagement" and becoming "friends" or "liked" by customers interacting across social media channels.

As we move into each new era, many elements of the previous persist. And, thus, some of the best elements of the previous eras will likely play important roles (perhaps forever) as we move into the seventh. It's not some binary switch that gets "turned on." As Harvard Business School professor Clayton Christensen said, in defense of the concept of digital disruption, *"This is a process, not an event."* [12]

That said, there is no doubt that a transformation is occurring.

The Trade Era
1850s–1900s

The Production Era
1900s–1920s

The Sales Era
1920s–1940s

The Marketing Department Era
1940s–1960s

The Marketing Company Era
1960s–1990s

The five historical eras of marketing are generally considered to have spanned from the Trade Era in the 1800s to the Marketing Company Era ending in the 1990s.

Consider a few data points—namely, that despite the huge, and in some cases, extraordinary efforts over the last 10 years to "*know*" and "*relate to*" our customers better through data, that:

- More than half of U.S. customers switched service providers in the last year due to poor customer service experiences—up 5% from 2012. [13]

- The rate of loyalty has barely budged among U.S. customers, rising just 1% since 2012, and customers' willingness to recommend a company rose by just 2%.[14]

- Only 23% of consumers say they have any relationship *at all* with any brand.[15]

- 75% of adult Americans say they prefer that their data not be collected or used at all by companies.[16]

A study conducted by the Corporate Executive Board in 2012 concluded that there is no linear correlation between the number of interactions with customers and the depth of relationship with that customer. Nevertheless, most marketing strategies center on this very metric: the more interactions we have, the more data we glean, then the deeper our relationship must be. It's simply not true.

As the Corporate Executive Board study noted:

> "*In reality, that linear relationship flattens much more quickly than most marketers think; soon, helpful interactions become an overwhelming torrent. Without realizing it, many marketers are only*

adding to the information bombardment consumers feel as they shop a category, reducing stickiness rather than enhancing it." [17]

Now, we're not saying that relationships are dead. Certainly, companies that have focused on customer relationships (Nordstrom and USAA are two well-cited examples) have been able to create differentiating strategies with a focus on relationship marketing. And there are many examples of best-in-class marketing organizations using social channels, content, data, and the mix of very smart, creative processes to develop deeper and more meaningful relationships with their customers. Some have reached that "evangelistic" stage of marketing.

But there is a shift happening. The data show that these relationships are "tenuous" at best. And brands are beginning to realize that it's NOT the product or service that the customer values, or that keeps them loyal—*it is the experience that they have at every stage of their journey with that brand.*

Content marketing, and creating content-driven experiences, has proven to be an extraordinarily powerful new way for marketers to create this experiential value for business. The idea of providing education, delight, and general usefulness (as a brand's approach to engage its customers) provides a new way to enrich interactions with customers at every stage of the buying journey.

The challenge before us is how to transform marketing from a subservient department that creates content only to describe the value of a product or service, into one that knows how to create, manage, and lead the development of valuable experiences over the next decade.

This is truly the way forward—and a step toward the answer to the question, "What do you *really* do?"

MARKETERS CAN CREATE DIFFERENTIATING VALUE

It's time to reclaim marketing's ability to create value. But that will happen only if marketing's goal is to create value that evolves customers from aware, to interested, to engaged, to sold—and then onward to loyal and evangelistic. The ability to deliver content-driven experiences consistently will be the single most important key to marketing's evolution along this trajectory.

Fifteen years ago, just as Trevor Traina was selling Compare.Net and the dot-com boom was in full swing, world-renowned marketing professor Philip Kotler published *Kotler on Marketing*. In it, he discussed the late 1990s—the period that fueled most of the thinking for his book—as a time of tumultuous change. But Kotler knew that this was merely the beginning.

Kotler concluded the book with a section called "Transformational Marketing," in which he discussed how the field would change with the "new age of electronic marketing." In the coming decade, Kotler wrote, *"Marketing will be re-engineered from A to Z. Marketing will need to rethink fundamentally the processes by which they identify, communicate and deliver customer value."* [18]

There's only one problem: 15 years have passed, and this vital transformation hasn't happened yet. It's time to get to it.

And this book is a step in that direction.

HOW THIS BOOK HELPS TRANSFORM MARKETING IN THE ERA OF EXPERIENCES

This book has been one year in the writing and five years in the making. Over the last five years, Robert and Carla have each worked directly with large enterprises in both the B2C and B2B space. After more than 100 workshops, advisory engagements, and in-depth meetings with businesses of all shapes and sizes, we've personally seen what is working and what isn't.

We've also watched as others have shown some terrifically productive thinking to help businesses scale the idea of content and marketing as well as the creation of customer-centric experiences. Their contributions are noted here and imbued into the suggested methodologies.

Let's be really clear: We are in the midst of a seismic shift in how products and services are marketed to customers. We wrote this book to help map out the future of the marketing department. In that regard, we believe:

- **Good enough is no longer good enough.** The classic goal of "creation of a customer" will simply be table stakes for marketing. The marketer's new objective will be to create differentiating and uniquely valuable experiences for customers that go well beyond the product or service.

- **Content-driven marketing IS the differentiating function of business.** Marketers must lean in, step up, and lead the business into the future. They must move beyond being a subservient on-demand production group built to service sales. Instead, they must lead the business as a strategic function that will enable the business to adapt to new disruptions.

- **We are entering a new, seventh, era of marketing.** Customers' experiences through all aspects of their journey with a brand will guide marketing strategy. Customers will be looking to be continuously delighted, surprised, informed, entertained, and assisted. They will seek out brands that align with their purpose and values. Relationships will continue to be tenuous, but will be deepened less on the quality of the product or service (or the quantity of interactions), and more by the differentiated experience *created within each interaction.*

In this book, we'll explore both the "why" and the "how" of navigating this new landscape. We'll put strategy before structure, function before form, and insight and creativity before action and activity.

We provide a suggested framework—a set of "better practices" (if you will), instead of "best practices"—for creating an active, functioning, and scalable way for marketing to use content-driven experiences to differentiate and create value. We call this new process Content Creation Management (CCM) because, as is true with any initiative (and in honor of William Deming), if we "can't describe what we're doing as a process, then we have no idea what we're doing."

To map our experience journey together, we've split this book into two halves.

- In the first half, we introduce you to this new era and discuss why it's vital for marketing to lead this new initiative and to earn its strategic seat at the table.

- In the second half, we provide a detailed look at the process of CCM and present an approach for:

o   How you might roll it out

o   How you'll need to communicate it

o   How you can build a measurement plan for it

o   How you can ultimately build a process that is
    adaptable and scalable

It's a journey for sure, and one for which we readily admit we don't yet have all the answers. This is as much an exploration for us, as it will be for you. Thank you for coming along for the ride as we chart this new map. As Confucius once said, "Study the past if you would define the future."

Let's go create the future of marketing together.

—Robert Rose and Carla Johnson, March 2015

ENDNOTES

1   http://www.foxbusiness.com/personal-finance/2014/09/17/eventbrite-millennials-driven-by-fomo-spending-more-on-experience-economy/

2   http://www.jwtintelligence.com/2013/01/data-point-constantly-connected-millennials-crave-sensory-experiences/#axzz39Be89ntb

3   http://www.v3.co.uk/v3-uk/news/1979635/microsoft-boosts-msn-portal-strategy-ecommerce-framework

4   http://www.adweek.com/news/technology/ifonly-sells-2000-experiences-its-first-year-158766

5   http://hbr.org/2014/07/the-ultimate-marketing-machine/ar/1

6   Ibid.

7   http://www.mckinseyonmarketingandsales.com/sites/default/files/pdf/Marketing%20Disruption.pdf

8   http://news.marriott.com/2014/09/in-an-industry-first-marriott-international-makes-bold-marketing-move-launches-a-global-creativeand-content-marketing.html

9   http://contently.com/strategist/2013/06/11/4-content-marketing-lessons-from-qualcomm-spark/

10 http://contentmarketinginstitute.com/2013/04/brand-content-media-transformation-case-study/

11 http://www.workforce.com/ext/resources/archive_mediafiles/Google_GSA_ROI_WP.pdf

12 http://www.businessweek.com/articles/2014-06-20/clayton-christensen-responds-to-new-yorker-takedown-of-disruptive-innovation#p2

13 http://newsroom.accenture.com/news/us-switching-economy-puts-up-to-1-3-trillion-of-revenue-up-for-grabs-for-companies-offering-superior-customer-experiences-accenture-research-finds.htm

14 Ibid.

15 http://blogs.hbr.org/2012/05/three-myths-about-customer-eng/

16 http://www.marketingprofs.com/charts/2014/25456/when-are-consumers-ok-with-brands-collecting-personal-data

17 http://blogs.hbr.org/2012/05/three-myths-about-customer-eng/

18 Kotler, Philip. *Kotler on Marketing: How to Create, Win, and Dominate Markets.* Part Four, Transformational Marketing. Free Press, 1999.

chapter 1:
WELCOME TO THE 7TH ERA OF MARKETING

"You can't connect the dots looking forward; you can only connect
them looking backwards. So you have to trust that the dots will
somehow connect in your future." | Steve Jobs

So, the first question is, why now?

Why is it so important for marketers to lean in, step up, and disrupt
classic modes of operating to create differentiating value through content-
driven experiences?

Look at our most recent past, and you can see entire industries and
professions being disrupted by the Internet and the web. Entire
business sectors such as publishing, retail, music, banking, and even
manufacturing have undergone seismic shifts. The pursuit of professions

such as photographer, journalist, travel agent, musician, and doctor has also gone through fundamental disruption.

Soon, literally trillions of connected devices will enable communication between companies and customers, and vice versa. 3D printers and new materials are enabling entirely new capabilities to produce products. If you don't believe that the same thing that has happened to photographers, journalists, and musicians won't happen to product and manufacturing companies, you are kidding yourself.

And marketing is changing, too.

MOVING TOWARD A 2020 CONTENT MARKETING PLAN

Today's powerful search engines, social network filtering, and ubiquitous mobile computing capabilities place powerful new tools in the hands of customers. A buyer's journey is no longer a straight line, not even static. People now can (and do) flexibly locate information, compare pricing, and make social recommendations about any number of competing solutions.

Customers are now savvier—simultaneously becoming researchers, publishers, reviewers, influencers, and experts on any manner of products or services. The ease by which information can be shared across the Internet, including mobile and social touch points, has required businesses to try to influence audience behavior by *increasing*—exponentially—the amount of content they produce.

Today, what generates interest, persuades, engages, and creates a sense of customer loyalty is the consistent engagement and unexpected delight in the experience that people have with the brand. In effect, today's marketers are in the business of being media companies—constantly informing, entertaining, and delighting audiences, while helping them to see that brands offer a differentiated *approach* to solving any customer need or want.

For marketers, it's simple: business as usual *isn't*. **Marketers shouldn't be acting more like media companies—they should BECOME media companies**. In a world where audiences are increasingly fragmented, the goal can no longer simply be about developing transactional relationships with customers; it must be about continuous engagement, passion, and loyalty. In short, marketers must focus on aggregating a passionate, loyal, and engaged audience, while developing content-driven experiences for long-term success.

So, yes, customers have fundamentally changed the way they browse, buy, and become loyal to the products and services they purchase. And it may seem strange, but we're now more than 20 years into the "digital disruption" that the Internet and the web brought to business. Guess what? People have already adapted to it, and remarkably so. Toddlers now routinely try to swipe print magazines, and are frustrated when the "screen" doesn't change. It's estimated that 36 cents of every dollar used for purchase is now influenced by digital content. And 84% of store visitors now use their mobile devices before or during a shopping trip.[19]

The 1989 movie, *Back to the Future Part II*, was set in the year 2015. You may be wondering where our hover boards are. Also know that the dystopian 1982 film, *Blade Runner*, is set in 2020.

Do you have a plan for 2020? It's a lot closer than you might think. By the time this book is published, you will be closer to 2020 than to a number of things we regard as the recent past:

- Your first Tweet—which could have happened in 2007

- Your first Facebook page or ad— which also happened in 2007

- Your first iPad—which launched in January 2010

So, 20 years into the digital disruption, isn't it about time we look for the next evolution of marketing? The web is no longer new. What's next?

Well, as Mr. Jobs so wisely said, we can't connect the dots by looking forward—we need to look back to where we've been in order to see where we are going. Let's step back and get some historical perspective.

THE SEVEN ERAS OF MARKETING

Most marketing textbooks generally agree that the development of marketing, as a process, occurred over five distinct eras covering roughly 125 years, with each era spanning roughly 20 to 30 years each. A sixth era, the Relationship Era, is commonly acknowledged (though not in all university textbooks) to be the current era, and began at dusk of the last century.

We believe we are now entering a seventh era, the Experiences Era, where the experience, rather than content, is king. But before we explore this new era more fully, let's put some context to the last 125 years.

The Trade Era
1850s–1900s

The Production Era
1900s–1920s

The Sales Era
1920s–1940s

The Marketing Department Era
1940s–1960s

The Marketing Company Era
1960s–1990s

The Relationship Era
1990s–2015

The Experiences Era
2015–????

The new, seven eras of marketing include the generally accepted Relationship Era—starting in the 1990s and lasting until today—and the new Experiences Era starting in 2015.

THE TRADE ERA: 1850s

You can hardly expect to even recognize marketing, as we understand the term, during this era. The Industrial Revolution that had already begun in Europe was just taking wing in the U.S. The 1800s was a century marked by invention and innovation in every aspect of business. Historians often call this the "market revolution," where the rapid development of manufacturing and advances in farming had huge effects on how people bought and sold goods and services.

This ad from 1885 touted Dr. Price's Cream Baking Powder and Flavoring Extracts.

This was a time marked by companies selling the excess of production. Whether large or small, companies were in the business of directly manufacturing a product (or harvesting one) and selling what they could through storefronts or marketplaces. Marketing in this era was characterized basically by manufacturers identifying the optimal places to sell and trade their goods.

Of course, advertising existed during this era and marketers were intent on describing the value of their products. For example, there's a wonderful ad for Dr. Price's Cream Baking Powder and Flavoring Extracts. Perhaps the most notable thing about the ad is that it feels compelled to tell you that the baking powder contains no ammonia, lime, or aluminum (was that really a differentiator in the late 1880s?). But also note that this product was available only where the company had storefronts (in this case, Chicago and St. Louis).

This focus on "availability," or "place" (as we start to build toward the classic four P's of marketing—price, product, promotion, and place) is what drove us to our next era.

THE PRODUCTION ERA: 1900s–1920s

By the time the 1900s rolled around, the U.S. economy was thriving and many were adapting to more urban lifestyles. Even though "advertising" had been around for many years, this is when the concept really exploded.

The Production Era was truly defined by the idea of mass production—and the public's fascination with the "science" of mass production. The idea that a company could set up factories to produce things in mass quantities and distribute them across great distances was simply amazing. Marketing and advertising, at that point, were focused on the idea of using this production and distribution capability as a differentiating asset.

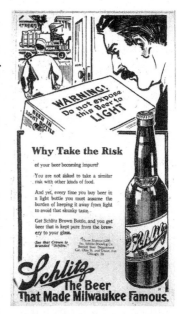

A Schlitz Beer advertisement from 1920 highlighted the features of the company's factory, which were a differentiator for their marketing.

Advertisements and marketing copy of the day would highlight how one company was the ONLY company with the ability to produce such a product in both quality and quantity, and why their manufacturing process was the best in all the land.

A 1920s ad for Schlitz beer summed this up well. The "secret," said the ad, was in the brown glass used in the bottles. Schlitz only bottled its beer in brown glass—and the windows in their factory also had brown glass—so the science was sound (or at least they said it was) and you could be sure your beer would be fresh.

Everything changed, though, on October 29, 1929, when the stock market crash known as Black Tuesday sent economic shockwaves all around the world.

THE SALES ERA: 1920s–1940s

If the 1920s were about optimism, boom economies, and the idea of distributing our amazing new "products" to diverse "places," the Sales Era was what brought a complete focus on "price" to the table.

> *"The man who will use his skill and constructive imagination to see how much he can give for a dollar, instead of how little he can give for a dollar, is bound to succeed."* —Henry Ford

The global depression affected almost every industry and its ability to produce products. Urban areas around the world (which had seen huge population growth over the last 20 years due to the expansion of heavy industry) were hit very hard. This, in turn, hit farming and rural areas and prices for crops fell by almost 60%.

At the center of this era was the salesman, and the focus on selling. In 1925, Bruce Barton wrote *The Man Nobody Knows,* a best-selling "how-to-sell" book that portrayed Jesus Christ himself as a successful sales executive. Then there was the enormously popular Dale Carnegie and his *How to Win Friends and Influence People,* which was written in 1937 and, to this day, remains one of the most popular business books ever written. Its main goal was to help you become a better salesperson.

Strategy during this era focused on *selling the product,* and price was at the heart of it. The marketing strategy was almost entirely based on "what you were getting" and "for what price."

The luster of overstated advertising had worn off, and the public was skeptical. They wanted to be *informed,* and have "proof" that what the marketer was saying was true.

A great example from the early part of this era is an advertisement for Pontiac. The company makes almost no effort to realistically depict the car, but focuses instead almost exclusively on the price and factual comparison of what you get for that price.

But, ironically, and leading us into the next era, the latter part of the Sales Era was marked by beautiful, artful advertising depicting the positive side of life. Led by the booming economy coming out of World War II, full employment, and a futuristic vision of the future, marketing was about to experience a renaissance.

A Pontiac advertisement from 1935 spotlighted the "what you get and for what price" focus of the Sales Era.

THE MARKETING DEPARTMENT ERA: 1940s–1960s

If you've followed the hit TV show *Mad Men*, you're familiar with the Marketing Department Era. Following World War II, and the ensuing economic boom, advertising agencies were all the rage and Madison Avenue was a glamorous place to work. The corporate marketing department was born—it was full of fresh-faced, business school graduates who studied the four P's and hired young Don Drapers to come up with pithy copy that would sell their products. It was all about careful product positioning:

> *"There isn't any significant difference between the various brands of whiskey, or cigarettes, or beer. They are all about the same. And so are the cake mixes and the detergents, and the margarines... The manufacturer who dedicates his advertising to building the most sharply defined personality for his brand will get the largest share of the market at the highest profit."* —David Ogilvy

This is when the creativity of marketing really blossomed—along with the three-martini lunch—and marketing and advertising became the most exciting parts of working in business. Cary Grant, playing an adman in an amazingly fitted suit, summed this up well in the film, *North by Northwest,* when he said to his secretary, *"In the world of advertising, there's no such thing as a lie. There's only expedient exaggeration."*

This was also the era during which two burgeoning technologies—television and computers—began to play a heavy role in marketing strategy. The first television advertisement in the U.S. aired in 1941: Bulova featured a plain picture of a watch face centered on an image of the U.S., and a voice over stated, "America runs on Bulova time." The whole thing lasted 10 seconds. This would, of course, drastically change things; it propelled companies to start creating "content" that was separate from their products. In no time at all, short jingles and animated characters that represented companies (as Ogilvy said) in a memorable way made their way onto the air and became the staples for many television campaigns.

Bulova aired the first television commercial in 1941. It was only 10 seconds long, but it opened up the world to marketers.

Computers, too, were introduced during this era. Now, for all but the largest advertising agencies, computers were prohibitively expensive. But whether they installed room-sized mainframes from IBM or subscribed to data from "computer services," the idea of using computers to segment target audiences and provide smarter strategies to reach customers flowered during this era.

THE MARKETING COMPANY ERA: 1960s–1990s

During this era, the focus was on the product. The question was always, "how do we sell the product?" But if you've watched *Mad Men*, you've probably noticed the ongoing conflict between Don Draper and his clients on how to develop something more meaningful than just "selling the product." In one episode, Don tries to come up with a new campaign for the new Kodak technology that will show slides.

"It's not a wheel. It's a carousel," he says. "This device isn't a space ship. It's a time machine."

It's this movement—to deeper, and (hopefully) more meaningful branding—that marks the transition from the Marketing Department Era into the Marketing Company Era.

In the late 1960s and 1970s the world became more global, and more complicated economically and politically. In turn, companies realized they had to stand for something more.

During the Marketing Company Era, the emphasis was on the *brand of the company itself*. What did the company stand for? As the decades progressed, the growing practice of being meaningful to the customer, and being "customer-focused" rather than "product focused," was challenged (for the first time) with the mass fragmentation of audiences. Cable television entered the home in the late 80s/early 90s, and due to the company-brand focus there was a shift toward niche marketing and target marketing to audience segments.

Perhaps no other communication strategy exemplifies this era more than Apple's iconic 1984 Super Bowl ad that featured a dystopian look at the future, and how Apple was "breaking us free" of the world of that dystopia. The ad was created by one of the new super agencies—Chiat/Day, based in Los Angeles—and the world of marketing became a competitive war to see who could best capture the feelings and emotions of a public ready to embrace what a company stood for.

Apple's 1984 advertisement wasn't about a product at all, but how an innovative company would set us free.

Then, in perhaps what might be considered "too neat" of a demarcation line, the year 1989 happened. We forget how transformative that year actually was. *Time* magazine called it "the year that changed the world." Consider that in just 12 months:

- The politics of Europe changed almost overnight. The Berlin Wall came down, partial democratic elections were held in the Soviet Union for the first time, and full elections in Poland and Czechoslovakia completely transformed the political landscape of those countries.

- Tens of thousands of Chinese students took over Beijing's Tiananmen Square in a rally for democracy. More than 1 million would eventually take part in the protests that would pave the way for democratic reforms and China entering the World Trade Organization 10 years later.

- Tim Berners-Lee and Robert Cailliau began work at the European Organization for Nuclear Research (CERN) on a new computer language for formatting, storing, locating, and retrieving information over the fledgling Internet. They would eventually devise what they called a "web browser" that could access the new "worldwide web."

- The Japanese stock market was at an all-time high, culminating a decade of Japanese economic expansion. Less than six months later, it would collapse and begin what the Japanese would later call "the lost decade."

Indeed, the world became much "flatter," to borrow from economist Thomas Friedman's metaphor that he popularized in the book, *The World Is Flat*. Along with globalization came outsourcing and offshoring, as the world itself became a more common marketplace. With this, differentiation across product, place, price, and promotion became even more complex as now, arguably, ALL of the four P's were replicable across the globe.

But a new trend was beginning to emerge: the move toward a more personalized relationship with the customer. Businesses were using customer databases for more direct marketing efforts in the 1980s. But, as the decade turned, a new technology phenomenon began to take hold of marketing: Customer Relationship Management (CRM).

While some argue that it was analyst firm Gartner that brought the acronym about, some credit Tom Siebel, the Oracle executive who would leave the company to form Siebel Systems, one of the first companies to truly focus on sales force automation and managing customer relationships. It was the dawn of what is widely known as the era we are now moving out of: the Relationship Era.

THE RELATIONSHIP ERA: 1990s–2015

In 1993, Don Peppers and Martha Rogers, Ph.D., wrote *The One to One Future*, a book that would change the landscape of marketing. In a 1996 reissue of the book, the authors ask (and answer) some of the seminal questions that would define the next 18 years of marketing strategy. They said:

> *"More and more companies have realized that interacting with customers is no longer an option, but a competitive necessity. And now they have questions: How should an interactive company treat its customers? What objectives should a business set for the interactions that take place at its site? How can it measure success? Should different customers be treated differently? Is it sometimes necessary to reward customers for participating in Internet dialogue?"*

Isn't it fascinating to see how many of those questions are still plaguing businesses almost two decades later?

Then, in 1999, Rick Levine, Christopher Locke, Doc Searls, and David Weinberger put forward a set of 95 theses and organized *The Cluetrain Manifesto*. This was during the time when the Internet and electronic disruption of the web was just getting its legs. In that book, the authors presented the notion of "markets as conversations." As Searls would state 15 years later in a conversation with Robert Rose:

"The Cluetrain Manifesto wasn't about marketing, it was about markets, and about how the power of consumers would fundamentally shift the relationship between buyer and seller."

Remember, they were writing this *before* the Internet and the web had erupted in any meaningful way.

But then, the dot-com boom made things, well, weird.

The Sock Puppet ad from Pets.com helped define the entire dot-com boom.

The late 1990s kicked off a wave of what could be called "postmodern" marketing. The dot-com bubble that lasted from 1998 to 2002 was marked by advertising and marketing content that seemed on one end to ridicule itself, with a blatant "over-the-top" self-referential style of brand messaging. One Super Bowl advertiser that became the symbol of the excess of that period was Pets.com and their spokes-sock puppet. What disco music and bell-bottomed jeans brought to the 1970s, the Pets.com sock puppet brought to this period. As Salon.com pointed out about this style of advertising in its after-market report in the early 2000s:

"The bottom line looks a bit like a gawking press coverage and a temporary surge in site traffic, but nothing so lasting that it could be called brand building, and nothing so irrefutably valuable that it could possibly justify the huge expenses for a whole patch of unprofitable companies." [20]

The over-the-top approach to marketing during the dot-com phase might have done more to hurt the practice of marketing than almost anything that preceded it. It's still a sore spot (sometimes quite literally) with companies, especially those that are heavily engineering-driven. The "Super Bowl commercial" is a running metaphor about the superficiality of marketing and how the marketer doesn't really focus on important things. Getting the dot-com "stink" off of marketing is one of the biggest challenges that marketing teams in larger organizations face today.

But still, like the Sales Era, the Relationship Era wasn't without its explosive success stories. In their follow-up book, *The One to One Manager*, Peppers and Rogers go through a number of case studies including one from First USA Bank, which was then the nation's largest issuer of VISA and MasterCard credit cards. Chase Bank acquired the company in 1997.

In that case study, the authors interview Richard Vague, then CEO of the bank, about his innovative customer acquisition program, "At Your Request." As Vague put it, the program was a "personal assistant, concierge, researcher, and travel agent, all in one." Vague's goal for First USA was that it would become a "trusted agent" for customers. It would do this by developing extended and personalized services that would make it hard to walk away when other credit card companies came knocking with lower interest rates. The company also added a reminder service called "Just-In-Time." This service allowed customers to fill out profile information for members of their family, including birthdays, anniversaries, doctor's appointments, and car repairs. The service would then send an email or fax to remind the customer.[21]

Remember, this program was being rolled out in the mid-90s. What seems to be "table stakes" for CRM these days was cutting edge for that time. Its goal was to develop more interactions with customers, so that the relationship would be closer and more intimate than with other credit card companies.

But, ironically, the First USA story also is a sign of just how difficult establishing "relationships" with customers can be. Once the "shining star" of a family of banks under parent company Bank One, First USA learned the hard way that simply establishing a relationship at the "acquisition" stage of the customer's journey doesn't always translate into great relationships after they become customers. By 2000, First USA's customer-service issues had resulted in a drop in stock price of more than 50%. By 2003, Bank One retired the brand.

Yes, even then, we began to see the importance of the experience across *the entirety of the customer's journey.* To paraphrase Jerry Seinfeld in an old episode of *Seinfeld*—in CRM, it's not only *acquiring* the customer relationship, it's *maintaining* it as well.

AND TODAY?

Of course, the Relationship Era continued after the dot-com bubble exploded, and some would say this era still survives. The early 2000s was marked profoundly by the rise of CRM software and a focus on delivering the "right message to the right person at the right time."

To supplement the CRM database, email relationship tools exploded onto the market in the mid-2000s. Social media began to get its feet wet with sites like MySpace and Friendster—each with tens of millions of members. There were books written on how to create marketing strategies for both of them.

Marketing automation software, built to leverage email and address delivery of content to known visitors to digital content channels, became the newest "must-have" capability of relationship marketers.

Then, as social media gained a real foothold toward the end of the first decade of the 21st century, the new focus became *conversations with customers* across the myriad media that they might be consuming. Social media became a key marketing function, as brands desperately tried to figure out how to deepen the relationship with an increasingly fragmented audience and a customer that was becoming more and more concerned about his or her data privacy and anonymity.

And that, of course, brings us to today—the early days of 2015.

EXPERIENCES: THE NEW ERA OF MARKETING

As we mentioned in the introduction, there can be no mistake now that over the last few years, content (and how a brand uses it) has begun to transform marketing strategies. Over the last five years, early-adopter companies such as Red Bull, Coca-Cola, Nike, American Express, and Marriott have made big bets—to the tune of tens of millions of dollars—on the idea that content-driven experiences will move their business forward.

It is in this context that we believe we are moving into yet a new era of marketing. It's what we call the Experiences Era. With hindsight, it's easy to see how each era moved into the next, and how some of them were doomed to be as short-lived as they were. So, while it's tempting to say that this new era will be better than the last, or any of the previous, the truth is that the Experiences Era may be as short as the Relationship Era, or it may, itself, be a transition to something completely different. The future is unknowable, of course, but by understanding where we've been we can better navigate where we're going.

So, when we claim to be moving into this new era of marketing, our contention is based on three fundamental arguments:

1. Customer Relationships are More Complicated than Ever

Similar to what happened during the transition from the Production Era to the Marketing Department Era, the ability of companies to differentiate based solely on the value and quality of their products has largely disappeared.

Now more than ever before, companies can easily reverse-engineer, produce, and/or copy features of existing products. These days, every industry seems to be going through some level of product and/or service disruption. From manufacturing, to consumer-packaged goods, to retail, to professional services, to healthcare, and so on, disruptive forces are reshaping the landscape for companies at the product and service levels.

Consider some examples:

- **Banks:** Lending Club, a new startup where customers lend each other money (as opposed to going to banks), has already brokered more than $5 billion worth of loans in five years.[22]

- **Light manufacturing:** Online marketplaces for 3D-printed designs already exist, and it is estimated that within five to seven years the minimum volume of production needed to enter a market will drop by 90%.

- **Taxi services:** New shared-car services such as Uber and Lyft have created better, easier experiences for consumers. In San Francisco, the taxi business has suffered a 65% loss in rides in less than three years.[23] Other cities such as Washington, DC, and Boston show similar declines.

It's a company's *approach* to solving customer needs or wants that differentiates the brand. Brand differentiation is no longer about product or service excellence—customers expect that. Today, it's the *experiential* gap that has widened. It's not enough to simply get the customer from A to B in a smelly old car. These days, the customer expects to be delighted at every interaction.

Now, whether Uber can actually continue to deliver that delight is another story. As this book goes to print, its competitors are already threatening to deliver better experiences.

Red Bull is a great example of a company that provides experiences. It doesn't differentiate on price (it's the most expensive energy drink on the market), product, place, or promotion (in fact, it has relatively standard distribution methods, advertising, and promotion budgets).

Where they spend their money and focus most of their effort is in creating differentiating, content-driven experiences that sear their brand and their approach into the minds of their customers. Whether it's extreme sports events, guys jumping out of space ships, a television network, or simply a magazine devoted to all things sports (which people pay to get), Red Bull creates valuable entertainment experiences that bond them to their audiences.

Companies such as Uber are disrupting the marketplace by providing the same service, but offer a more valuable approach and experience.

The real magic in the Red Bull strategy is that they could probably sell anything they want. They have such a strong brand and bond with their audience that if they started selling clothes, surfboards, or even bicycles, they'd probably succeed.

So now it is up to marketers to **go *beyond the relationship* that a customer has with a product or service**, and instead develop deeper, more meaningful experiences for them, whether or not they have an existing relationship.

2. The Democratization of Content and Experiences

As mentioned earlier, it's not only products that can be created and duplicated, it is content as well. Publishing and distribution tools now make anyone a mass publisher and brand that must be dealt with.

Much has been written about our human capacity to absorb the vast amounts of content that are being produced on a microsecond basis. But from the invention of the printing press, there has always been more content than any human could consume. The "consumption ceiling" was reached long, long ago. However, as technology enables more powerful and better "filters" to the content aimed at buyers, the marketer must develop something more compelling in order to rise above the noise. Yes, a brand can pay for an ability to rise above the noise, but it cannot pay to have more relevance and value.

This is not simply an advertising mandate; this is an everything-the-company-communicates mandate. Simply paying for attention will no longer do. We, as marketers, have to hold it long enough so that WE matter to them.

Consider investment company, TDAmeritrade, which focuses on clients that are interested in trading stocks. Once the customer is acquired, the company provides them with access to their thinkorswim.com community and signs them up for *thinkMoney*, a print magazine. The goal of this content-driven experience is to continually engage traders (after they become customers) and empower them with the right tools, tips, research, and capabilities to trade more effectively. They've learned that subscribers to the magazine trade five times more than non-subscribers.[24] That's something that will never be delivered with a paid advertisement. It's a valuable experience, separate from the product that creates a more engaged and frequent customer.

3. The Adaptation of the Marketing Department

Businesses tend to look at the developments of marketing trends with a focus on both hardware and software development. In other words, we look at the development of tablets, or mobile phones, or refrigerators with screens as yet another platform that we need to account for. Or, we see new customer aggregation points, such as broadcast television, cable TV, Facebook, Twitter, LinkedIn, Snapchat, or even Ello as software platforms to which we need to assign special content teams and content strategies.

The result over the last 15 years has been the creation of silos, even within marketing departments. We now have social teams, mobile teams, social CRM teams, e-business teams, web teams, PR teams, brand teams, and so on.

It's simple: businesses must realize that there will be no possible way to scale to every channel on which they must ensure the brand story is being told.

It is vital for marketing departments to stretch and create valuable content across the entirety of the funnel, because that content can (and will) be shared by customers. That's the only way a brand can ever hope to be on as many channels as is necessary. **Every valuable experience or content that is shared by audiences across a social network reduces the need of that brand to maintain presence on that channel.**

Thus, the only way to scale is to adapt the marketing department's structure and purpose around the creation, management, and ultimate flow of information (i.e., content) to both describe and, more importantly, *create value* for customers.

And this must happen despite existing or future channels. In short, marketing departments must implement new organizational changes that meet the fast-changing needs of customer empowerment and the need for the organization to orchestrate the vast amounts of content it produces.

The description of value is relatively well understood. There is no doubt that marketing departments are producing exponentially MORE content than ever before to describe the value of their products and services. It's the CREATION of valuable experiences and content that is the new muscle for most organizations—one that we hope to exercise and develop a bit with this book.

Ultimately, these three arguments explain why everything must change about how we go to market. But this isn't a new prescription. Sixty years ago, during the Marketing Department Era, Peter Drucker wrote:

> *"The purpose of business is to create a customer. The business enterprise has two and only two functions: marketing and innovation. Marketing and innovation produce results. All the rest are costs. Marketing is the distinguishing, unique function of the business."*

This is just as relevant today as it was back then. Yet somewhere along the way, in one of the eras, this idea got lost. Today, it's time for marketers to claim it back. Marketing *can be* the distinguishing function of the business, but only if its goal is to continually evolve customers.

Marketing has to be built in order to *create* value, not just describe it. We're classically trained as marketers to describe value across the four P's. Now, we must do more by creating value using both content AND experiences.

As we said earlier, it's not enough for brands to just act like media companies. They must *become media companies* that develop and delight audiences continually. As media companies, brands engage customers through every aspect of the marketing funnel:

- From their first awareness of the product, service, or brand promise

- Through their nurturing and decision-making process

- To when they become customers

- To when they become loyal, up-sold, cross-sold, and ultimately evangelistic about subscribing to our brand approach.

Most marketing departments in large enterprises still operate either in the Relationship or Marketing Department Era. In some companies, marketing is a service organization that views the sales department as a "customer" and exists simply to support sales with the materials they need. Even worse, in some companies, marketing is an annoyance that just creates pretty brochures while the "important work" happens elsewhere. In some companies, content (and the creation of it) is seen simply as busy work for marketing when there are no brochures to produce. For many, this won't change and their inaction will be fundamental in their demise.

But some companies are, indeed, changing. At Kraft, for example, content-driven experiences fuel the creation of more effective advertising. Kraft understands its customers at an unprecedented level, drawing out more and more insight into their preferences, behavior, and how to delight them.

For other companies, like marketing automation software company HubSpot, content creation and publishing are as important as product development. Dharmesh Shah, co-founder and CTO of HubSpot, has been quoted as saying, *"Content is as important as code."*

In this new era of marketing, unique, impactful, differentiating content-driven experiences will become as important as product development. Successful marketers will adapt and change in a constantly evolving media operation that focuses on creating delightful experiences to inform, entertain, engage, and evolve the customer.

Welcome to the seventh era of marketing—*Experiences.*

KEY CONCEPTS IN THIS CHAPTER

- Most marketing textbooks agree that the development of marketing, as a process, occurred over five eras covering roughly 125 years, with each era spanning approximately 20 to 30 years each. A sixth era of marketing, the Relationship Era, is commonly acknowledged (though not in all university textbooks) to be the current era, and began in the late 1990s. During the:

  o Trade Era—the focus was on bringing surplus goods to market.

  o Production Era—a company's ability to mass-produce products became a differentiator.

  o Sales Era—marketers concentrated on persuasive language and price to sell products.

  o Marketing Department Era—marketers focused on the four P's (product, place, price, and promotion) and tried to differentiate by making products "aspirational" and "desirable."

  o Marketing Company Era—products were a piece of a larger solution that companies offered.

  o Relationship Era—companies developed one-to-one and deeper relationships with customers through more relevant communications.

- We contend that we are moving into a seventh era of marketing, called Experiences. This is based on three fundamental arguments:

  - The customer relationship is more complicated than ever. The Internet has fundamentally shifted customer expectations about their relationships with brands, making those relationships more complex and delicate than ever.

  - The democratization of content means that in addition to our competitors, everyone who creates, shares, and publishes content competes for our customer's attention.

  - The adaptation of the marketing department in the business is providing an opportunity for companies to differentiate through content. But this means that marketing must be more strategic, and take a more holistic view of the entire customer experience.

ENDNOTES

19 http://www.deloitte.com/view/en_US/us/press/Press-Releases/
    e051ee4e0e395410VgnVCM1000003256f70aRCRD.htm

20 http://www.salon.com/2000/05/03/super_ads/

21 Rogers, Don and Peppers, Martha. *The One to One Manager: Real-World Lessons in Customer Relationship Management.* Crown Business, 2002.

22 https://www.lendingclub.com/info/statistics.action

23 http://www.web-strategist.com/blog/2014/09/24/disruption-from-the-collaborative-economy/

24 http://www.agorapulse.com/blog/content-marketing-strategy-joe-pulizzi

chapter 2:
MARKETING WITH A CAPITAL "M"

"We keep moving forward, opening new doors, and doing new things, because we're curious...and curiosity keeps leading us down new paths." | Walt Disney

Did you know that the chief marketing officer (CMO) is a modern invention? Just five years ago, only 23 of the Fortune 100 companies even had a CMO as the head of marketing.[25] Compare that to the title of CIO, a function that has been around since the early 1980s. As computers made their first appearances on the desktops of modern businesses, executives quickly recognized the CIO as an overall business strategist.

The CMO title itself seems mostly to be an invention that grew out of the mid- to late-1990s and the dot-com exuberance that kicked off the Relationship Era. Many of the new marketers that joined these startup technology and media companies gave themselves this title. In fact, you might argue that it was the dot-com era that relaunched the idea of "marketing as business strategist." Up until that time, the marketing function solely focused on generating demand for products. The resulting implosion in the early 2000s is something that the practice is still living down. As we mentioned in the previous chapter, walk into any engineering-driven technology company and the scorn that older engineers have for marketing "weasels" can be palpable.

But, arguably more than any other business function, both marketing and technology have changed the go-to-market approach for every single business. From the marketing perspective, the challenge in connecting with customers is harder and more competitive than ever. As a result, the required strategic vision and tactical skill sets differ dramatically from what was required just a few years ago.

Social media, the empowerment of customers, and the demand for corporate transparency are redefining brands and threatening the control (if control even exists any longer) of brand messaging. If you think about who does what within today's business, marketing and sales serve as "promise makers" of customer experiences, and the rest of the employees serve as "promise keepers." The promise keepers have influence over whether customers believe we have kept our promises or not. Therefore, as marketers, we have to expand the scope of what we do and whom we influence. But, we also must make sure that we align internally and externally.

In short: it's no longer good enough for marketers to simply generate leads to our sales people, foot traffic to our stores, or visitors to our ecommerce site.

MARKETING'S ROLE IS MUCH MORE CRITICAL AND MUST:

1. Evolve a customer from the first time we meet him or her

2. Turn curious browsers into engaged prospects

3. Turn engaged prospects into qualified buyers

4. Turn qualified buyers into satisfied customers

5. Ultimately, turn satisfied customers into loyal brand subscribers.

If we don't deliver on these five critical roles, we risk the financial consequences of confused, disappointed, and frustrated customers.

THE NEW MARKETER: EXPERIENCE CREATOR INSIDE AND OUT

For the last decade, people have talked about changing buyer behavior. Yet, little has changed in the marketing department's view of our role in creating customer experiences. We're the people who should orchestrate the entire customer journey—creating the experiences that companies have with customers and the employees who serve them—but we don't.

We intellectually understand that the days are gone when marketing simply served as a brand steward (or cop, depending on your point of view), created fluffy awareness campaigns, and held events. Now, beyond the legacy functions of making every communication effective for selling, marketing *must help lead the transformation of how business is done*. But, we must do more than just intuitively understand this transformation because it requires marketers—from CMOs to young professionals—to *actually develop new competencies and mindsets to thrive as leaders in new and expanded roles.*

The changes in buyer behavior have forced changes in how we think and act as marketers. Those marketers who thrive on uncertainty feel like kids on summer vacation, leaping at the variety of opportunities, ideas, and inspiration. Apprehensive marketers hold onto traditional practices, thinking that if they ignore the disruption, they won't have to address it. Fear of the unknown freezes their openness. In between are those just trying to keep their heads above water, or searching for "permission" from their C-suite to try something more strategic. Yes, we marketers still yearn for influence within our organizations and scrape for dollars and resources. But, it's a catch-22. We have to prove ROI on every investment we make and continually push for the value we think we deliver, while we beg for the power to innovate to do just that.

It's time to step forward and assert our authority. In order to gain influence and earn our seat at the "big kid" strategy table, we need to quit thinking like marketers and transition into becoming customer experience leaders who understand the view and strategy of the entire organization; because, if we continue to limit our role to one of "mere" communication, or as a "service agency" to sales, we won't be able to transform organizations or the way marketing operates within them.

Research by The Fournaise Marketing Group found that 73% of CEOs think marketing lacks credibility. In contrast, 69% of marketers think their strategies and campaigns have an impact—they just don't know how to prove it. [26] They aren't equipped to have a marketing conversation in the context of what impact they can have on business performance. Much of this disconnect between marketing and CEOs derives from marketers not understanding the strategic and leadership roles we must take on.

This struggle doesn't apply purely to marketers in the trenches. In its research report, "The Transformative CMO," The Korn Ferry Institute points out that to become "transformative," marketing executives must understand how the marketing function intertwines with every other function within the company.[27] To be successful, these executives need to drive enterprise-wide change in an increasingly complex and unpredictable *business* environment. Take Kathy Button Bell, CMO of Emerson. In her position, she has infused marketing's role into that of human resources, product development, IT, and customer service. She sees her role as building collaboration across the enterprise and simplifying how the business operates. To do that successfully, she points out the need for marketers to get exposure to other functions and understand how they all work together.

> *"Our biggest trend for 2014 was the elevation of marketing,"* said Button Bell. *"It's changing, and we're doing things that aren't traditional for the role of marketing. We're responsible for the integration of external and internal conversations. We focus on empowering customers. The only way to drive customer experiences is to drive integration across the enterprise. And the only way for marketers to do that is to understand the business, and then simplify it. Everything we do at Emerson is about simplification."*[28]

LIVING IN BETA

Here's something to consider. Analytics, by its very nature, means we are looking in the rear view mirror to see where we are going. So, while it's great to have context of where we've been, and learn from our failures and successes, we're also charting new roads here. By the time we've witnessed, experienced, and documented a best practice, our customers have often moved on. Our nemesis isn't our perceived competitors—it's our customers' short attention spans. In order to think creatively about how we capture and keep their attention, we have to think differently about the role we have within our organizations.

Modern marketers struggle with incredible change, but the pressure to do so is only getting greater. Recently, Forrester Research and the Business Marketing Association released findings about the expanding role of marketing. Ninety-seven percent of marketers said they expect the pace of change in marketing to accelerate, and 76% felt their leadership evaluates success or failure more rapidly than ever before. Other findings included the following:

- 21% of marketers say the skills for which they were hired are now obsolete

- 97% see a dramatic increase in the breadth of marketing skills needed

- 97% are doing things they've never done before

- 45% can't find marketing candidates with the right skills.[29]

Tim Kopp, then CMO of ExactTarget, summed this up well in a 2013 CMO.com interview when he said that the successful CMO of the future will *"not only be chief marketing officer, but chief customer officer, head of strategy, and change agent in chief."* [30]

There is a constant demand for new skills and added resources. But if CEOs aren't seeing our worth, and we're not able to prove that worth, how do we function in a new landscape? The only way to "prove" worth in this context is for we marketers to step up, take risks, and expand our leadership roles and influence at the same pace as our levels of responsibility increase within an organization.

We need to lean in. We need to become strategically bold about our capabilities and our responsibilities. We need to become comfortable living and working in beta because that's where our growth lies—trying new ideas, testing new approaches, and thinking unconventionally. When marketers can move elegantly into these strategic shifts, ambiguity and uncertainty will be seen as opportunities, rather than liabilities.

It's time we become more innovative in how we think. That requires us to examine our perceptions about marketing's role and how we can lead change. But here's the kicker: We can't convince executive leadership of the value we deliver to an organization unless we believe it ourselves and walk the walk, i.e., demonstrate that value.

Rather than take the safe route, marketers must sit at the executive table and lead strategic conversations about the growth of their organizations. They need to become comfortable with both accountability and change, becoming more agile in the process.

Great marketers step beyond their areas of responsibility and transform their organizations. They spend a great deal of time understanding the operational and financial details of their company, while immersing themselves in the world of their customer, gaining insights and perspectives. They're perpetually curious, which makes it easier to transition from a tactical marketing role to that of a trusted advisor and strategic partner at the executive level.

MARKETERS AS GROWTH DRIVERS

So, yes, we agree—marketing *should be* a vital growth function that takes any company to new places, connecting the dots in valuable ways, creating a thread between legacy thinking of the past and innovative insights going forward.

To do that, marketers must insert themselves into the overall corporate strategy. We need to make it clear that we're not just the idea people; we must be part of the group that *stays* in the room to get the work done. Marketers must be the ones who can have intelligent, strategic conversations with IT, sales, product development, human resources, finance, and the rest of the organization. It's hard. But, in order to lead transformation, we have to put our heads down, roll up our sleeves, and hold ourselves accountable alongside everyone else.

For marketers to truly transform organizations, we have to go beyond asking, "What's the role that marketing *could* have?" to ask ourselves, "What role *will* marketing have in OUR organization?"

Here are some examples of the new role of marketing:

- For five months, Antonio Lucio, global chief marketing and communications officer for Visa, had human resources report to him, during which time he tightened the relationship between the company's strategy and how employees were recruited, developed, retained, and rewarded. *"I fundamentally believe that there is one brand and one narrative, but you have multiple stakeholders that you serve,"* he shared. *"Although everyone talks about it, and it's intuitive to do, it's important to approach your employee audience with the same attention and rigor that you do with external audiences."* [31]

- Eduardo Conrado, Motorola Solutions' senior vice president – chief innovation officer, now holds responsibility for both marketing and IT. He's able to move IT from back-office support to an integrated approach to creating systems of engagement with marketing. *"If you're able to invest in systems of engagement,"* said Conrado, *"then IT becomes a point of differentiation in the marketplace. IT helps us get closer to the customer."* [32]

Marketers have a set of tools and skills that allow us to drive change. We also have a front-row seat from which we can watch the continually changing landscape of customer expectations and monitor the need for driving outcomes. By stepping beyond what our peers see as our traditional functions, we become valued advisors and trusted leaders within the company.

MARKETERS AS UNIFIERS

As we expand marketing's role outside the wall of "just marketing," we can bring people together by building non-traditional teams that collaborate to solve customer problems. This means we'll have to learn what motivates each group and then develop a compelling vision as well as superb communication and integration skills. In order to unify, we have to serve as advocates of innovation; we must help people understand the greater vision and then we must serve as the point-people when those team members execute the work. Change can't be addressed tactically. Instead, we have to think strategically about how we create and lead experiences that fascinate and inspire audiences to take action—both inside and outside of the enterprise.

"People judge you on the totality of how they experience the brand," said Linda Boff, executive director, global brand marketing for GE. *"There are many things that aren't traditionally part of marketing brand that now matter in how you show up. If your marketing is good but your product is bad, then that means your marketing is bad, too."* [33]

By thinking of ourselves as unifiers, we'll gain a holistic view of what needs to be done and an understanding of how to integrate processes to drive growth. It's important to understand the key relationships for marketing, but it's equally important to understand how everyone is interconnected throughout the organization. Thinking like a unifier will demonstrate real business results that align across the enterprise, and marketers will take on a measurable role in generating revenue, and creating new and different customer experiences.

Too often, when talk turns to the details of how to get the work done, marketing stands up and leaves the room. We don't know what to do, we're uncomfortable, and there's plenty of work waiting back at our desks. That has to change.

The classic scenario works like this: human resources asks us to give a public relations spiel to new employees. Great...we show up, give our 15-minute talk, and we're done. There's no consideration about how our presentation (from an external marketing perspective) translates into what new employees hear as a first impression of the company. Is what we discuss from a customer experience perspective the same thing that these employees can expect now that they're part of our team?

Here's how it should work: marketing sits down with human resources and talks about what human resources is *really* trying to accomplish with new employees. People who work in human resources aren't communicators; marketers *should* be. So how do we unify the message and the experience between the brand and new employee on-boarding—and ask how we extend the brand story through human resources so that the people who we recruit fit our culture, believe in our purpose, and seamlessly step in and begin creating delightful experiences for our customers? How do we reach them in new and meaningful ways based on their generational preferences? How and when do we need to bring IT into the picture so that the experience the candidates have is easy and skips the typical online frustrations and black hole of bureaucracy?

We must be willing to stay in conversations longer, dive deeper into what, strategically, needs to be accomplished, and bring our unique skills to the table. It's our ability to set a vision and close the gap between that and the current reality of what actually "is" that adds value. By helping people understand what *could* be, how all the puzzle pieces fit together, we're taking off the blinders and helping groups understand how to work together to create new and different experiences. It's our opportunity to use diplomacy and stellar interpersonal skills to help bring ideas to the table and build confidence in our new approach to old challenges. We can facilitate collaboration while still owning part of the process and the outcomes.

MARKETERS AS INNOVATORS

One of the newest responsibilities for marketers is that of spearheading inspiration. It is our responsibility to see where the world is going and to help our companies get there before the world does. We must look for opportunities to incubate ideas in small ways. Once we understand where our world is headed, we can translate that understanding into practical direction, inspiration, and executable actions.

The marketing environment has changed so dramatically in just the last few years that many people are fearful. That fear leads them to taking the safe route with their careers and their corporate initiatives. The result is the delivery of uninspired work by professionals who struggle to function in a new, changed environment. This squanders opportunities and fuels the perception that customers have of "noise in the marketplace." Instead, we should be thinking "future forward" and lead from the future. If we know what we want our organizations to look like by 2020, how do we back that into today and start laying the groundwork for that change?

In his book, *Escape Velocity: Free Your Company's Future from the Pull of the Past,* Geoffrey Moore explains how the things that made a company successful in the past can be the same things that hold it back from going forward in the present.[34] Marketing's history of task-oriented roles, product launches, lead generation, and media hits are often the culprits that can hold that past in place, frustrating forward progress. That has been a big factor in Barnes & Noble's inability to understand the digital landscape of its business. While the company held onto the brick-and-mortar mindset of how customers buy books, they're flailing because they can't keep up with Amazon. Instead of reinventing their business (and marketing) model, they're putting a bandage on the real problem by partnering with Google for delivery.[35]

We have to reconsider how we can serve as a seamless conduit through all parts of the organization to set the strategic direction required to free our companies from the practices that hold them back.

Our impact on the business is "transformation." It's all about transforming how marketing is organized and functions, how we integrate with and lead others, and how we get customers to view us. We have to be responsible for building our credibility. We must shed the idea that growth comes only with perfection, because perfection is impossible to achieve. Instead, we must give ourselves permission to fail while in the process of innovating. As long as failure scares us and keeps us from trying new ideas, we'll never be able to unleash the energy, passion, and contagious enthusiasm that organizations need in order to transform.

As we marketers learn how to lead with inspiration, we'll strengthen our ability to generate new breakthroughs and help others develop more creative vision. We'll be able to push boundaries by leaning into creativity, mental agility, and liquid processes.

MOVING FROM PRODUCTS TO EXPERIENCES

To grasp the concept of moving from products to experiences, we have to understand purpose. By understanding and infusing the experiences that we create for customers with a shared brand purpose, we create critical moments of truth about what our brand truly stands for, rather than what we're trying to sell. BMW understood this decades ago when they quit talking about gas mileage and power windows, and instead about the *ultimate driving machine*. Dove talks about how to have real beauty rather than how great their soap cleans. Marketers who first focus on "purpose" ultimately engage, delight, and inspire customers.

Newton's first law of motion states that an object at rest will stay at rest until an external force acts upon it. It also says that an object in motion will not change its velocity unless an external force acts upon it.

The powerful forces of our customers' changing behavior and expectations are only now beginning to move us off dead center. But, we're still behind. It's time to change the vector and velocity. Beth Comstock, CMO of General Electric, talks about the need for perpetual motion marketing—marketing that's continually in motion and evolving, rather than the "one and done" mentality. What do vector, velocity, and perpetual motion have to do with our behavior?

In a *Harvard Business Review* article titled, "Rethinking The 4 P's," Richard Ettenson, Eduardo Conrado, and Jonathan Knowles discuss how to refine the four principles of marketing: product, place, price, and promotion. Developed in 1960 by Edmund Jerome McCarthy, a marketing professor at Michigan State University, the four P's no longer reflect today's customer behavior, particularly in the B2B world.

During a five-year study (which they describe in the article), the authors found that the four P's model fell short in three important ways:

1. They stressed product quality and technology (even though these are now table stakes for doing business);

2. They failed to spotlight the value of solutions; and

3. They distracted from taking advantage of opportunities to serve as trusted advisors and strategic partners.

In contrast to the four P's, the authors introduced a new framework, Solution, Access, Value, and Education (SAVE), that looks like this:

- **S**olution: Instead of *product,* the focus is on *solution.* Define offerings by the needs they meet, not by their features, functions, or technological superiority.

- **A**ccess: Instead of *place,* the focus is on *access.* Develop an integrated cross-channel presence that fits customers' entire purchase journey, instead of individual purchase locations and channels.

- **V**alue: Instead of *price,* the focus is on *value.* Talk about the benefits relative to price, rather than stressing how price relates to production costs, profit margins, or competitors' prices.

- **E**ducation: Instead of *promotion,* the focus is on *education.* Provide information relevant to specific needs at each touch point, rather than relying on generic advertising, public relations, and personal selling.[36]

In order to SAVE ourselves and evolve our marketing mindset, we must let go of our outdated approach to marketing. We need to take the business objectives we're trying to move forward and think about different frameworks and approaches that might get us there. It's clear that our traditional product structure isn't moving our business strategies forward. Therefore, we must reevaluate how we function because structure should always follow strategy.

| Instead of PRODUCT | focus on **SOLUTION** Define offerings by the needs they meet, not by their features, functions or technological superiority. |

| Instead of PLACE | focus on **ACCESS** Develop an integrated cross-channel presence that considers customers' entire purchase journey instead of emphasizing individual purchase locations and channels. |

| Instead of PRICE | focus on **VALUE** Articulate the benefits relative to price, rather than stressing how price relates to production costs, profit margins or competitors' prices. |

| Instead of PROMOTION | focus on **EDUCATION** Provide information relevant to customers' specific needs at each touch point in the purchase cycle, rather than relying on generic advertising, public relations and personal selling. |

The SAVE model reflects the approach marketers need to take to create conversations with audiences around solving problems, rather than selling products or services. Credit: Motorola Solutions and *The Harvard Business Review*

MARKETING FORWARD

Our only continuum is one of change. But constant change creates fear because we don't have a "normal" to use as a baseline reference. However, without someone (or something) to compare ourselves against, how can we know if we measure up? The old measuring devices no longer work, so we have to look at what we do as a form of perpetual motion. We have to evolve every day: learn, iterate, and repeat. Technology certainly helps us do this faster.

However, marketers aren't changing as quickly as the tools we use. There's a wealth of information about the problems facing us, but only a trickle of insights from companies who actually have gotten the ball in motion and have momentum behind it. To get there, we need a proactive mindset: a willingness to learn, get uncomfortable, and accept that "normal" no longer exists.

To elevate marketing to the leadership position it deserves within our organizations, we must be able to articulate the value that we're able to create. Because, until we can elevate the dialogue about what we do and how we can impact the business—i.e., how we can maneuver the new environment—we're doomed to remain as order takers, tacticians, and undervalued overhead.

Now is the time to scan the horizon and discuss what *could* be. What's our story as a marketing profession? Knowing that story is the only way we will be able to prepare—today—for the skill sets, demands, and expectations of what companies need to create agile environments capable of shifting with changing customer expectations.

In order to lead companies and industries, we marketers must first understand how to lead our own profession. How will traditional processes hold up under this time of transition? Without the willingness to have these conversations, we're perpetuating a hidden force that undermines our work: legacy thinking. It is easy, when under pressure, to default to what is comfortable. The pull of the past is hard to resist. That pull is so strong that it makes it hard to change thinking, processes, and outcomes. If we're ever to come into our own as a profession and leaders within organizations, though, it's time that we step out of our comfort zones.

THE ROAD AHEAD

This is an incredibly exciting time to be in marketing. We're in the midst of redefining our role from the communication and brand people toward the pathfinders who evolve business. We have the ability to restructure how we function and contribute to the greater growth of the companies for which we work. Our profession has a vital role in driving business, integrating teams, understanding customers, connecting with employees and, ultimately, creating the experiences that woo and capture audiences.

This is *our* time. Let's make it remarkable.

KEY CONCEPTS IN THIS CHAPTER

- Marketing's role must expand beyond the traditional responsibilities of managing the brand and generating leads. Marketers must now create audiences and evolve buyers into satisfied customers and loyal brand subscribers.

- While buyer behavior has changed dramatically, marketing has not kept pace. Our inability to establish credibility and exert authority hinders our ability to drive change within our organizations.

- Much of what we do as marketers expands outside of tactical skills and falls into three areas across the enterprise:

  1. Growth drivers—marketers must insert themselves into the overall corporate strategy. To do this successfully, we have to understand business goals and objectives and then establish marketing as a vital role within the organization.

2. Unifiers—marketers have the ability to bring cross-functional teams together to engage customers and solve their problems.

3. Innovators—as the group closest to the customer, marketers have a responsibility to see where the world is going and then help our companies translate that into practical direction, inspiring ideas and executable actions.

- The SAVE framework shows how marketers can shift their mindset from one of products and features to one of solving customer problems. It updates the concept of the four P's into **S**olution, **A**ccess, **V**alue, and **E**ducation.

ENDNOTES

25   http://blogs.hbr.org/2012/05/three-myths-about-customer-eng/

26   https://www.fournaisegroup.com/Marketers-Lack-Credibility/

27   http://www.kornferryinstitute.com/reports-insights/transformative-cmo-three-must-have-competencies-meet-growing-demands-placed

28   Interview with Carla Johnson, December 12, 2014.

29   http://solutions.forrester.com/Global/FileLib/Reports/B2B_CMOs_Must_Evolve_Or_Move_On.pdf

30   http://www.cmo.com/articles/2013/4/30/the_future_of_marketing.html

31   Interview with Carla Johnson, December 19, 2014.

32   Interview with Carla Johnson, November 24, 2014.

33   Interview with Carla Johnson, December 16, 2014.

34   Moore, Geoffrey A. *Escape Velocity: Free Your Company's Future from the Pull of the Past.* HarperBusiness, September 2011.

35   http://www.fool.com/investing/general/2014/08/11/sorry-the-barnes-noble-and-google-partnership-wont.aspx The Motley Fool, accessed November 25, 2014.

36   http://hbr.org/2013/01/rethinking-the-4-ps/ar/1

chapter 3:
THE CASE FOR CONTENT CREATION MANAGEMENT

"What lies behind us and what lies between us are tiny matters compared to what lies within us." | Oliver Wendell Holmes

What are "experiences" and why should marketers manage and deliver them?

These might seem like obvious questions, but they deserve to be asked, because the phrase "customer experience" still seems to lack a common definition. Ask all the analysts, software tool providers, consultancies, and agencies out there, and you'll get a variety of divergent proclamations about what "customer experiences" are, the best way to deliver them, and why, of course, they deserve to be managed carefully.

None of this helps those who need to understand it most: we marketers who are responsible for navigating our businesses through change and creating optimal customer experiences. How ironic that these analysts, agencies, and software companies haven't created an optimal customer experience in their efforts to communicate what it means to deliver that very "experience."

We need to understand this change—and fast. If we don't, we run the risk of running down the same familiar road we've been on since the early 2000s. Digital is a disruptive medium. Therefore, we figure, it must be separate and distinct from other experiences. Businesses of all sizes have spent the last 15 years separating out the idea of digital versus physical. Brands now have vice presidents of digital marketing that sit in offices adjacent to vice presidents of what? *Regular* marketing? They have CRM teams and social teams, who sit beside the web teams. These people work with the ecommerce teams, but somehow don't get along with the blog teams, who have love/hate relationships with the PR teams. And then there's the traditional agency they've engaged, along with their super-hip and forward-thinking digital agency. The result? A structural mess.

So, with that said, let's get an inevitable scope problem out of the way first.

A SHIFT IN FOCUS

We most certainly are NOT the first authors to talk about the "customer experience." Very much like the approach of content marketing, businesses have been thinking about customer experience management (CEM) for some time. Even as far back as the Marketing Company Era, the idea of "customer experience management" was a popular topic. It is defined as the "totality of the customer experience." And, thus, every single customer experience can be considered part of that thinking. By that logic, setting a price is part of CEM; the interaction that the customer has with the owner's manual is part of CEM; and choosing whether to make the product from wool or cotton is part of CEM.

To suggest that the totality of CEM is marketing's sole responsibility is not our intention.

To be clear: In this book, we are discussing only a subset of CEM. **We examine only those content-driven experiences that help evolve a customer through his/her journey from aware, to interested, to committed, to loyal, and ultimately, to evangelistic. In most cases, the value delivered from these experiences will actually be separate and distinct from the product or service itself.**

Marketing is transforming from a group that creates its value by describing the experience the customer will have with the product or service being offered. Instead, new marketing strategies must focus on creating experiences that deliver value that goes beyond the product or service.

In order to do that, marketing must evolve and create new processes.

THE PROBLEM OF MARKETING'S NON-RESPONSE TO CUSTOMER EVOLUTION

As we've discussed, market realities have changed the ways that customers now become aware, browse, investigate, purchase, use, complain, and/or become loyal to a brand. However, the business processes that facilitate awareness, shopping, differentiation, use, and service have not changed. To date, the legacy approach has been to throw teams and technology at all the individual stratifications of the funnel, and to create ever more campaign-based efforts to optimize each stratum.

The force of this legacy approach is strong enough to encourage service providers and agencies to do exactly the same. Many brands use different agencies for different slices of their business. Even big agencies now have a "direct group," "digital group," "experiential group," and "loyalty group." This has significantly reduced the value that agencies are providing to their clients. Tom Goodwin, CEO and founder of The Tomorrow Group, brilliantly summed up this trend in a recent article in *The Guardian*. He concluded:

> *"We've created the long tail of marketing, where each campaign has ever smaller budgets, ever shorter lifespans, diminishing aims, all so wonderfully cheap in execution, so wonderfully proficient in terms of outputs, but so entirely pointless. It's this maintaining excitement for a Twitter feed of 4,000 people, or keeping 500 subscribers on YouTube happy, that is the marketing of our time. It may be cheap, but it's a pointless distraction and it's not solving any of the problems that are keeping our clients up at night."* [37]

And this is the key challenge. Marketing departments are currently working separately to highlight the company's value by creating more digital experiences than ever before. What must change is the structure of the strategy that delivers a cohesive, connected, and consistent portfolio of experiences that integrates everything a brand does (physical or otherwise) to help create the *total customer experience.*

We propose new, valuable content experiences, which should be created and managed by the marketing team. They *will be part* of and ultimately enhance the total customer experience. But, they will offer separate and distinct value from the product. They should not be created like a campaign, nor as content has always been created (as a response to a new offering), but rather like a product itself.

THREE CORE COMPONENTS OF THE CHANGE IN PROCESS

In our work, we've seen a number of high-performing brands start to think about content, marketing, and experiences in a new way. Three skill sets, or competencies, are common among these companies, and can provide a strong business case for a new process (or approach) to be put in place.

They are:

1. **Orchestrating Events, Not Guiding Journeys**

   Experiences are not paths or journeys. They are events consumed in a nonlinear fashion. Regardless of whether it's a long, high-touch B2B journey, or a completely transactional B2C journey, customers don't want to be guided; they simply expect to be charmed at every step, and on their own terms.

2. **Meaning-Driven, Not Data-Driven**

   Data, by its very definition, has no meaning. It's just a collection of facts and statistics aggregated for reference or analysis. To make data meaningful, businesses must develop new strategies to find that meaning. Instead of looking for proof-of-life within the data, they must instead ask insightful and honest questions—and look for the data to substantiate or disprove the hypothesis.

3. **Organizing for Agility, Not Speed**

Much has been made about the need for marketing departments to be more agile—but it's not necessarily about moving faster. The inability to find the calm out of the chaos, and the constant pressure of "more" is due to a fear of moving too slowly. Rather, marketers can find joy in the balance of creating customer-centric experiences and reorienting to more agile strategies.

Let's look at each of these.

1. ORCHESTRATING EVENTS, NOT GUIDING JOURNEYS

The buyer's journey will no longer be a guided tour.

A lot of digital ink is spilled on how businesses should map their digital content platforms to the buyer's journey. To be clear, this is still a worthwhile function. Marketers need to realize, however, that the map shouldn't be drawn to increase the number of mile markers that guide customers through the brand's ecosystem of marketing and content experiences. It is, rather, to establish the right *balance* of experiences. The goal, in fact, should be to provide the *least* amount of conversion friction between the customer, the desired action, and the value to the customer's purpose.

Yet because of the ease with which businesses can create and publish new content platforms, marketers have taken the classic lesson of "reach and frequency" to absurd levels in some cases. Every siloed group now maintains its own "content" platforms for its small slice of the buyer's journey. Teams are rewarded for the number of interactions they can create with a customer—with a flawed notion that this drives a deeper relationship between the customer and the business more broadly. In fact, it's usually quite the opposite.

In one study, The Corporate Executive Board Company examined the impact of stickiness across more than 40 variables, including price, brand, and how often customers interacted with the brand. They found that the single biggest driver of stickiness in the funnel, by far, was "decision simplicity."[38]

WHEN LESS IS MORE

The Singapore Tourism Board aimed to deliver a customized and optimized user experience on its signature site, www.yoursingapore. com. What normally would consist of multiple microsites, video-sharing channels, and informational sites all managed and measured separately, would leave the seams of internal silos and processes showing. The Singapore team knew that it needed to integrate multiple audiences, multiple regions, and multiple platforms into a contextual, targeted, and emotionally connected portal. Seamless, frictionless content and optimal experiences became the function and the strategy.

By creating as *few interactions* as possible and ensuring clear and intended impact of each, you create in your customer the *desire* to experience more. In short: it's not about more marketing, more content, or more experiences. It's about how the business creates the most valuable experience, infused by a digital strategy at only the right opportunities. Brands should resist the urge to send more and more "valuable content" down the throats of beleaguered customers, lest they find they are making the buying experience entirely more complicated and harder to manage than it needs to be.

YourSingapore.com has reduced the number of experiences to create a simpler and higher impact experience. Credit: www.yoursingapore.com - Screenshot accessed: 12/15/2014

Key Learning:

High-performing brands are developing balanced portfolios of digital experiences that map across the buyer's journey, are integrated across both physical and digital channels, and feature many different content types. These companies structure their experience portfolios to benefit the customer first and to benefit the delivery mechanism of the content second. Many have created specific cross-functional teams that are organizing both physical and digital content platforms, as well as architecting ways to integrate these experiences.

2. MEANING-DRIVEN, NOT DATA-DRIVEN

Facts don't change beliefs.

The roles of the CMO and CIO continue to evolve. The use of content and data to enhance customer experiences is one of the primary drivers of this evolution. But data alone is just a series of meaningless raw numbers that often distract from the real issues that may be at play. Consider how many times data is used to measure "proof of life" for a new marketing team or technology that has been put into service. That team has every incentive to manage its performance without regard for, and sometimes even in competition with, the other marketing teams and technologies.

The classic example here is the separation between sales and marketing teams in B2B organizations, where the "digital experience" can be entirely different once the "hand-off" is made. But across all types of organizations, it's not uncommon for marketing teams to build walled gardens where data and measurement are held prisoner to the goal of the team.

Data and digital experiences become meaningful when they generate true, actionable insight. In isolation, data are theoretical answers to problems the business probably doesn't understand. And experiences alone are simply creative projects or performance art. Meaning emerges when experiences are infused with the insight and contextual optimization afforded by data. The infusion comes from creative, insightful questions that are designed to improve the process, not prove the point.

THE BEAUTY OF THE RATIONAL AND THE EMOTIONAL

Wilson Raj, global customer intelligence director at SAS, framed this elegantly when he said, *"Data, while powerful, is only half the story. The other half is an understanding of the emotive needs of our customer. What are their aspirations, fears, dreams, desires, etc.?"*[39]

High-performing businesses are balancing both the rational and the emotional to optimize the digital experiences they are creating for customers.

Consider Kraft Foods Group and what Julie Fleischer, director of data, content, and media (an important title to note), is accomplishing with the merging of these concepts. As one component of a completely integrated experience (including a print magazine, packaging, website, social, email, and video), Fleischer and her team track more than 20,000 attributes of some 100 million annual visitors across the experience. That is 2 trillion pieces of data being assimilated over the course of a year. The company has merged both its data management and content platform; it uses the data to provide insight into how to address the purchased advertising that Kraft does through its media buying. This has enabled the company to get quadruple the ROI from its creation of an integrated digital experience than from ad buying alone.[40]

It's important to distinguish between an analytics problem and a data problem. To quote Wilson Raj again:

> *"CMOs must ask, 'Do I have the data?' If the answer is 'yes,' but I can't get at it, I don't have a Big Data problem. I have an analytics problem. But, if the answer is 'no', then the CMO must start to examine where they can get it and add in the missing linkages."*

This is a critical factor for both the CMO and CIO. To properly ask, "Do *I have the data?*" the business must first know the answer to *"what data is needed?"*

In order for data to have more value for a business than does existing information, marketers need to get beyond using analytics as a method to "prove" success or ROI. Instead, marketers must use data and measurement to derive more meaningful insight to develop fewer, but more beautiful and powerful, experiences for customers.

> **Key Learning:**
>
> High-performing businesses are developing new leadership roles on the marketing team. (Fleischer's title is one that may become more common.) These managers are creating strategies that peel back the layers of big data to make it manageable and meaningful. They aren't necessarily scientists or mathematicians, but they know how to ask the right questions about the data, customers, and influencers to glean insights that move the business forward.

3. ORGANIZING FOR AGILITY, NOT SPEED

Quick is a measure of time; fast is a measure of speed.

Agile is a term that all the marketing kids are dancing to these days. But what often gets lost in translation is the difference between being fast and being agile.

Undoubtedly, the digital disruption has left many marketers struggling to rediscover the joy in their profession. Recent studies have found that 66% of CMOs feel pressure from their CEO or board to prove that marketing has value. Another 60% say their leaders are "turning up the heat."[41]

Moreover, marketers are feeling pressured to become developers of digital experiences. In a study that surveyed the Global 1000 businesses on how they were reorienting their operations to manage the "modern, always-on, and mobile shopper," 96% said that integrating digital media components has fundamentally affected their business. Sadly, a third of the marketers in these business said these shifts have *"left them feeling 'under pressure and vulnerable.'"*[42]

These are keen observations. The fear of moving too slowly is causing marketers to do foolish things and to develop *more* experiences and digital content rather than optimize a set of well-defined digital experiences.

High-performing organizations are finding that "more and faster" is the wrong metric and that they must step out of it. As they evolve beyond the old, stale hierarchies and processes of the last 100 years, these companies are changing the way they infuse experiences intelligently into every part of the customer journey. Put simply: They are reorienting to agile strategies, not fast strategies.

As the number of potential digital experience opportunities explodes, businesses must resist the urge to be everywhere all the time, and instead focus on being in the right place at the right time.

Key Learning:

The "social conversations" and "real-time" experiences being created today should not be an unrelenting "have you heard us yet," and then three seconds later, "we SAID, have you heard us yet?" Rather, the goal for high-performing organizations should be a permanent state of agility ... of *we'll be there when YOU need/want us to be.* In other words, it's not how fast the push notification arrives every time the customer is out for a jog. It's more about having the ability to quickly send that perfect piece of media WHEN the customer asks for it, either by direct request or through an automated preference.

Understanding the difference between being agile and moving fast brings the joy back to the process of marketing.

REDESIGN MARKETING FOR CREATING CONTENT EXPERIENCES

It's simple: Marketers *must* get beyond the cycle of chasing campaign-oriented capabilities around every emerging channel. To succeed, marketing departments must evolve.

They certainly must be able to *describe the value* of the product or service through various campaign-focused offline and online content islands such as television, print, social, and mobile. But, they must also *create differentiated experiential value* that is separate and distinct from that product or service, and then integrate the physical and digital world seamlessly.

This new focus beyond the campaign means that content can no longer be everyone's job and no one's job—a collaborative effort is required. **The creation, management, publishing, and promotion of content-driven experiences must become a strategic function in the business.** This new focus beyond the campaign requires that content be made real. Content can no longer be simultaneously everyone's job and no one's job.

To accomplish this, new processes must be created, along with new roles to facilitate those processes. This is an approach or methodology that focuses on the creation of content-driven experiences as a separate asset; it has as much potential value as any given product and could potentially have revenue possibilities. We call it Content Creation Management.

KEY CONCEPTS IN THIS CHAPTER

- We are making a business case for content-driven experiences, not the totality of the customer experience. The distinction is important.

- There are three key concepts to our case for Content Creation Management:

    1. Marketers now must focus on orchestrating events, not guiding journeys. The buyer's journey is growing ever more non-linear, and it will be impossible for marketers to scale to meet every new channel. Thus, marketers should simplify, and focus on creating fewer, high-impact experiences that customers want to share.

    2. To derive true meaning from data, businesses must develop new strategies that ask honest, insightful questions that improve the process, not prove the success of campaigns or teams.

    3. Marketing departments must reorganize around agility, not scale. Today's challenge is not to be "everywhere we can." It is to be "anywhere we need to be." Thus, teams should be

centered on creating differentiating content versus content that is structured around platforms or technologies.

- The new focus should be on content as a strategic function in the business. Thus, the creation, management, publishing, and promotion of content requires its own strategic function. We call this Content Creation Management.

ENDNOTES

37   http://www.theguardian.com/media-network/media-network-blog/2014/sep/04/advertising-agencies-dying-marketers-challenges

38   http://hbr.org/2012/05/to-keep-your-customers-keep-it-simple/ar/1

39   Interview with Robert Rose, June 2014.

40   http://adage.com/article/best-practices/kraft-content-drive-broader-marketing-effort/294892/

41   http://www.marketingcharts.com/traditional/2-in-3-cmos-feeling-pressure-from-the-board-to-prove-the-value-of-marketing-36293/

42   https://econsultancy.com/blog/65351-96-of-enterprise-businesses-feeling-the-pressure-of-digital-transformation#i.19dz5w915ufdfu

chapter 4:
ORCHESTRATING THE EXPERIENCE:
NEW BUYERS AND THEIR JOURNEYS

"If you don't know where you're going, any road will
get you there." | Lewis Carroll

What is a "buyer's journey?" Do our customers really go through some
kind of predictive path on their way to buying a product or service? Has
this *really* changed over the last decade?

Customers are definitely more informed than they used to be; that's no
surprise considering all of the technological tools at their disposal. But
have the reasons *why* they make the decisions they do fundamentally
changed?

We contend that, no, they haven't changed. Marketers must still appeal to customers' personal values and purpose. And yet, marketers still segment buyers by things that lack real relevance to the purchase decision. As Theodore Levitt, one of our greatest marketing professor heroes, once said, *"People don't want to buy a quarter-inch drill. They want a quarter-inch hole."*

In their article, "Marketing Malpractice: The Cause and the Cure," Clayton M. Christensen, Scott Cook, and Taddy Hall eloquently added to this idea:

> *"Instead of trying to understand the 'typical' customer, find out what jobs people want to get done. Then develop purpose brands: products or services consumers can 'hire' to perform those jobs."* [43]

With the explosive growth of content marketing and the emphasis on targeting influencers, segmentation has become more complicated. Marketers are now targeting "audiences" by using the same flawed practice of targeting buyers by demographics; they are separating them by physical profile rather than by their purpose, or by what they find valuable.

WHY THE TRADITIONAL SALES FUNNEL NO LONGER WORKS

One of our biggest challenges as marketers is that we can't predict how customers will actually behave. Any success we have stems from the experiences we've already designed. As a result, we spend our time trying to improve the efficacy of these experiences and create new ones to replace the old ones.

Further, in order to improve these experiences, we break them up into layers of our sales funnel. The logic goes "we got X many leads from this initiative, so we should do more of this," independent of how valuable it was to the customer. This certainly makes it easier to manage from our end as marketers—and in a world with a small number of ways for us to design experiences, this feels like a tenable strategy. But, because today's omnichannel world offers so many ways for customers to move through a buying process, focusing on the traditional sales funnel is no longer realistic.

For starters, the idea of the sales funnel is incredibly outdated. In 1898, Elias St. Elmo Lewis came up with the idea of the purchase funnel, which we tend to call the sales funnel.[44] To get there, Lewis spent a lot of time studying the advertising profession. What he saw was the need to create sound practices in advertising that could apply to many industries.[45]

Lewis's musings and writings led to the AIDA model—attention, interest, desire, and action—that many marketers still use more than 100 years later. There's just one problem: Buyers have changed over the last 100 years, and they will continue to change. That's especially true as we see content playing a bigger and more important role in creating the experiences that influence how people make decisions.

The problem is this: Far too many marketers and companies are still using mid- to late-20th century hierarchies, strategies, and processes.

Gary Vaynerchuk of VaynerMedia said it well: *"Market in the year you're actually living in."* That means you have to create and deliver content and experiences that are relevant for today, and be agile enough to respond to how audiences want them delivered in the future.

With mountains of information instantly available at a buyer's fingertips, customers now create their own journeys. They educate themselves. But here's the thing: *self-educated audiences don't necessarily mean well-educated audiences.*

In the last few years, we've changed how we think about the process of creating experiences for customers. SiriusDecisions introduced us to their Demand Waterfall™ model, giving us a framework to measure and benchmark demand generation from a B2B buyer's initial inquiry up to the close of a sale. The Demand Waterfall™ brings together the efforts of sales and marketing in the process.

McKinsey's Customer Decision Journey model showed us how messy, complex, and interconnected the buying process is, and why buyers don't logically flow from one decision to the next. Instead, we realized that buyers make decisions and then revisit them, adding and deleting the brands they consider along the way.

One of the big advantages of McKinsey's model is that it's circular, rather than linear. Prospects don't come in at the top of a funnel and drop out the bottom. Instead, they move through an ongoing set of touchpoints before, during, and after a purchase.[46]

SiriusDecisions Demand Waterfall™

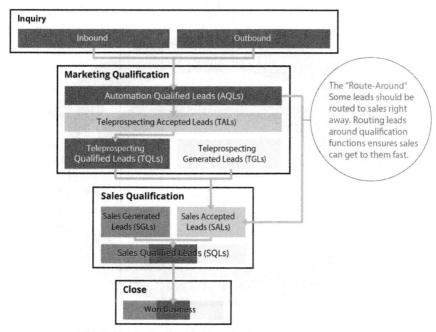

1 Inquiry

Best-in-class organizations distinguish inquiries that come from inbound and outbound sources.

2 Marketing Qualifications

The second phase of the waterfall shows the work that needs to be done to get leads ready for sales.
- AQL represents the critical system-generated qualification stage.
- TAL calls out the first key handoff of demand.
- TQL indicates a prospect ready for sales attention.
- TGL pinpoints leads created by "small-net fishing" and cold calling.

3 Sales Qualification

The third phase adds leads that are generated by sales or partners, making for a complete demand waterfall.

4 The Close

Our final phase shows the ultimate result of opportunities from all three primary sources.

Demand originated from marketing-led activities   Handoff from one function to another

Demand originated from teleprospecting function   Demand created by direct sales or channel resource

The SiriusDecisions Demand Waterfall™ gave marketers a framework to measure and benchmark B2B demand generation. Credit: SiriusDecisions

McKinsey & Company Consumer Decision Journey

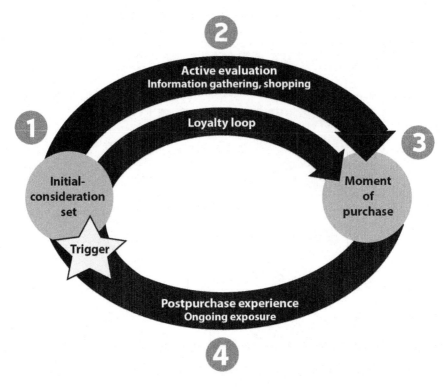

The consumer considers an initial set of brands, based on brand perceptions and exposure to recent touch points.

Consumers add or subtract brands as they evaluate what they want.

Ultimately, the consumer selects a brand at the moment of purchase.

After purchasing a product or service, the consumer builds expectations based on experience to inform the next decision journey.

The McKinsey Customer Decision Journey recognized the nonlinear process that customers use to make decisions. Credit: McKinsey & Company

The good thing about the Customer Decision Journey model is that it recognizes the back-and-forth and repeated efforts that buyers go through. We've all seen buyers who seem indefinitely stuck in a particular stage, fearful of making any kind of a decision, which includes saying, "no thanks."

So, what's the bad?

> *"The problem is in the name itself. Brands may put the decision at the center of the journey, but customers don't. Jonathan Becher, CMO at SAP, believes that for customers, 'the pivot is the experience, not the purchase.' The Customer Decision Journey might be circular, but if the focus is still on the transaction, it is just a funnel eating its own tail."* [47]

This is the critical point: **People now experience a brand many times and in many different ways—and many of these experiences come from sources outside of the brand.**

That's the most important thing that marketers forget about how today's customers buy: It's the experience that matters most, and it's the experience that creates the pivot point. People can be huge fans, significant influencers, and advocates even if they've never been (and maybe never will be) a customer.

Take Tesla, for example. In 2014, the starting price of a Tesla car was around $75,000. Equipped with location-based suspension, real-time traffic-based navigation, commute advice, and a smart calendar, it's not a brand you'd tap if you only need a vehicle to get from point A to B. But, unlike other luxury car manufacturers, Tesla has a huge following of people who will never buy one of their models. Why are these people fans? Because Tesla believes in creating a long-term sustainable society that's weaned from fossil fuels.[48]

Do these people matter if they're not buying a car? Absolutely, they do.

In fact, Tesla believes so much in the need to build a sustainable society that they've accelerated the development of technology for the industry. How? One way is that they allow anyone who wants to use their patented technology in good faith to do just that. They realize that their biggest competitor isn't the electric car, but rather the huge inventory of gasoline-powered cars manufactured every day.[49]

Marketers who focus on just the people involved in the buying process miss a huge opportunity to create influence and emotionally engage large audiences. If you think that brand advocates are only customers, you're missing out on the power of social influence. This influence matters a great deal in our digital world; companies can no longer guide buyers by the hand and expect them to end up with their product or service. Marketing has to "set the scene" for buyers AND influencer audiences to have delightful experiences at *every stage* of today's nonlinear journeys.

CONTENT-DRIVEN EXPERIENCES, NOT COMPLICATED GUIDED JOURNEYS

When you start to take this outlook on the buyer's journey, it makes sense why we need to stop supporting a sales-and-marketing-driven process. If we approach it from this perspective, we miss the nuances of how people actually buy, and instead, base our efforts on how enterprises sell. When we organize content around a sales process, we get locked in and don't think about how buyers make decisions in the real world.

What we *should* be doing is shifting our focus toward a content-driven experience process. Understanding the buyer's experience is vital. Customers have a decision journey and our processes need to reflect that.

Most marketers, however, overcomplicate this. We buy into mapping the customer journey and then get overly enthusiastic about detailing and providing a layer or conversion metric for every move. Yes, we need to understand the buyer's process. But we need to think about the scale that we use to map it. How many times, in our consulting work, have we seen a marketer's "buyer's journey" as a series of two dozen conversion points—and some kind of campaign-focused content program to facilitate a decision at each one? The net result is that the brand doesn't understand how to prioritize, and ultimately creates two dozen mediocre experiences, as opposed to any that are high-impact or deliver true value.

Micro-mapping theoretically gives you more details, but it also creates a bigger problem for marketers unprepared to execute on it compared to not mapping at all. Without a journey, we're clueless as to where customers go. With too much detail, we're so overwhelmed that we spread resources too thin when we have to try and cover them all. As a result, we end up creating average (or even negative) experiences in total.

The marketer's role is to find a happy medium. We should be creating a balanced portfolio of appropriate, relevant, and high-impact experiences at ONLY the stages of the buyer's journey where we can be most influential and deliver the most value.

To say that we can "guide" a buying process across every decision point with content isn't true. Buyers will do what they want and we lack enough control over that process to be able to guide them.

Instead of trying to force people into a next step of a complex process that *we've* created, we must create experiences that are so mesmerizing and valuable that buyers *want* to take the next step, and then we make it obvious what that next step could be. Along the way, we have to look at how our content is performing and how well it's creating the right experiences for our audiences.

One of the biggest roles that marketing has taken on in the last few years is to reach audiences in the moments that influence their decisions the most. For example, when you look at a product on Amazon, they show you what others also bought along with that particular item. They know you're already in the buying mode, and they know what you're interested in, so they're creating an experience that makes it easy for you to take the next step.

Let's look at how Visa mapped its customer engagement journey and shifted from being transaction-centric to focusing on the holistic customer experience.

When McKinsey introduced the circular Customer Decision Journey model, the Visa team recognized characteristics in its own business.

"Through changes in the omnichannel world, we saw that we needed to move away from transactions (swipe of a Visa card) to a full value-added experience in which transactions were one component of the consumer journey," said Antonio Lucio, global chief marketing and communications officer for Visa. *"There were experiences before, during, and after the swipe that we were realizing through research and trends. When we saw the McKinsey research, we knew it was time for us to look at things more holistically."* [50]

When Visa transitioned to a new CEO in late 2012, they began looking at how they could maintain the vibrancy of their brand over the next 10 to 15 years. They realized that they needed to make some fundamental changes, particularly with how they evolve consumers (B2C side) and merchants (B2B side), in order to create deeper relationships with them. To do that, they needed to explore how they could create a holistic and integrated consumer experience.

Lucio's team started by studying the data they had on customers, and how and when Visa interacted with those customers.

"We have 2.5 billion accounts on file, which is more accounts than Facebook and Google combined," explained Lucio. *"We saw that we had significant opportunities to combine our data with that of our merchants and issuing partners, and then combine it with the data that we had from Facebook and Google. It allowed us to create a more informed, richer decision journey that brought to light more points of opportunities for engagement with Visa."* [51]

During this process, the team looked at how a typical U.S. consumer would go about researching and booking a vacation to Mexico. They considered each point in the process (e.g., reading reviews on TripAdvisor, asking for input from their social networks, shopping prices, and making reservations online), as well as how the consumer would make decisions regarding entertainment and dining choices during the vacation.

Using research and data, Lucio's team was able to map a rich customer decision journey. Visa now had the critical interaction points and could drive more transactions into the business.

"I wouldn't say that we have this completely figured out," added Lucio, *"but as we evolve through a better and richer use of data, our model is going to*

become more robust and iterative, especially as we're able to cross more data with our clients, Facebook, and Google. We'll be able to easily test different messages at decision points and make sure that they are the right messages. This is how we'll continue to move from transactions to a comprehensive consumer experience. [52]

STOP ORGANIZING MARKETING AROUND SOFTWARE AND HARDWARE

Marketers tend to get caught up in new platforms and technologies and build strategies around them. We now have a Facebook strategy, a LinkedIn strategy, and a mobile strategy. With the exponential growth and simultaneous decline of channels, this strategy is untenable. Brands will never be able to keep up with the next "new thing" in terms of marketing channels. And by assembling teams to focus solely on channels, brands will over-rationalize efforts to keep them viable well after the usefulness of the channel may have run its course. We would never consider having a "print marketing team," so why should we have a "mobile marketing" or "Facebook marketing" team?

Instead of pursuing independent, siloed strategies, we must examine the bigger picture of how customers consume content and what they experience in the process. We know that certain experiences inspire people and make them want "more" change as they get deeper into the engagement journey. How can we make the buyer experience more effective in these phases of the decision-making process?

Think about the process rather than the form. Stop trying to nail down content specifics for each stage. We need to better understand how we can react to what an audience needs, so that we can respond to any situation. We need to think about the experiences we're creating with each of our channels. How do we use content to deliver those experiences? Forget about ROI for a moment; this isn't about generating tons of traffic—it's about using compelling content to create conversations.

Vail Resorts does a great job of this with its EpicMix program. The EpicMix ski pass connects subscribers to an online and mobile app that captures the experience of snowboarders and skiers on Vail Resort mountains. People can track their vertical feet climbed, earn pins, post to social channels, share photos, track ski and snowboard progress, and join racing competitions.

Vail Resorts understands that customers expect relevant content and touchpoints across every area of the organization and through every channel. Your customers are no different. Each of their experiences—from your website, to phone conversations, to live chats, brick-and-mortar stores, to Facebook posts—must be consistent.

It's time to move away from the sales funnel and the customer decision journey. Instead, we must think about creating experience-driven touchpoints that go beyond the products or services we sell. We can't restrict our efforts to what drives immediate sales leads, because that limits what we can do. Don't focus on persuading and promoting in order to sell. Rather, think about enabling and empowering experiences.[53]

The Michelin Green Guide series is a long-lived example of how to create a meaningful experience for an audience, whether or not they're customers.[54] What does Michelin sell? Tires. What is the experience they create? That of a travel partner. If you want to know about ferry tolls, sites to see, great places to eat, or find a hotel in your budget, the Green Guides have you covered.

DEVELOPING AUDIENCE PERSONAS

Who, exactly, are we creating these experiences for?

We hear marketers time and again say, *"We know who our audience is."*

Our next question is always: *"But do you?"*

Marketers file many things in their heads. Buyer personas are usually one of them. While we think that we know who our buyers are, going through the process of developing personas is one of the pillars in the content creation process. You have to know *whom* you're addressing before you know *what* you should be saying. Otherwise, you have no idea what matters to them and what you can say that delivers value to them.

In a world where customers are inundated with information and marketing messages, focusing on personas is key to capturing your audience's attention. Not only do you need the attention of your audience—which you may or may not be able to get—you need the attention of the people who influence them.

THE ATTENTION ECONOMY

In the 1970s, marketers began trying to engage customers in new ways. Anyone remember McDonald's collector glasses? Go back far enough, and you can find Ronald, the Hamburgler, Mayor McCheese, Officer Big Mac, Captain Crook, Grimace (the purple blob that stole milkshakes), and other fun characters you could add to your everyday dishware.

Companies were looking for new ways to connect with customers when they weren't in front of the counter or a sales person. We were in the infant stages of tapping the customer's attention, during a time when they received a mere 500 marketing messages per day. Marketers were beginning to ingrain brands in our head, programming us to remember them and to connect emotionally. That marked the beginning of the shift from pure promotions to more subtle branded content.

Twenty years later, Google stepped in. It was 1997. The Packers won the Super Bowl, *South Park* was in full swing, and *Titanic* won 11 Oscars. Companies were upping the ante by now, almost doubling the number of marketing messages that customers received each day.

Today, we see 10,000-plus marketing messages from the time we wake up until our heads hit the pillow. They span more platforms more aggressively than ever before. Brands relentlessly try to grab our attention. We see TV screens when we get into a cab, get pop-up windows in our web browsers, and hear ads when we're on hold for the dentist.

The double-edged sword comes with the ease we have as publishers to generate content. We have an immediate opportunity to reach people, but so do our competitors. Today, it's the experience that matters. We not only have to *grab* the attention of the audiences that matter to us, we have to hold it long enough so that *we matter to them.*

To matter to our customers, we have to know them better than they know themselves. We have to study their problems, understand their pain, and predict where they need to go in the future. We can no longer simply play defense against what our competitors say. Instead, we must deliver value that leads customers where we know they need to go.

Often companies use the voice of the customer to decide what content they'll create. But what they don't realize is that if they're asking customers what they think, and then listening online for what they do, they're just getting the same information as are all their competitors.

Your job is especially challenging in the B2B world where statistics say that 67% of the customer journey is digital.[55] Even worse, Corporate Visions points out that up to 60% of those sales situations end in "no decision," meaning that customers stick with their current situation.[56] They don't believe the value of change overshadows the risk of staying with what they have, the known enemy.

Therefore, we have to go above and beyond what customers are telling us they want, and understand them so well that we can see blind spots they don't know they have—just as Visa has done by understanding the holistic picture of consumers and their engagement journey.

WHO IS YOUR AUDIENCE?

Marketers need to realize that the buyer persona isn't always the same as the audience persona. One of the goals of content marketing is to attract attention, and we're trying to capture that attention and hold it. But we're not always able to get direct access to buyers and influence them in ways that we'd like. When that's the case, we have to look at the broader audience: who are *all* the people involved in the decision-making process and who influences them? If you can't reach the buyer directly, reach the people who influence them.

Take, for example, the audience for a university's marketing efforts. At first glance, you'd probably say that it's two groups: students and their parents, the people who actually "buy" from the university.

But a much bigger audience actually influences the decisions that the students and parents make about where to go to school. These might include alumni; professors and other staff; local and state businesses that hire interns and graduates; the government (local, state, and federal), because it impacts things such as tuition rates and student loans; nonprofits that contribute through fundraising; sports franchises that support athletic teams; and so on.

Take a minute to think about one of the main personas for your company. Who's your top buyer? Now list all of the people—*all of them*—who might influence that buyer somewhere along the line. It could be someone in purchasing who checks references. It could be their administrative assistant, who's a gatekeeper. Or, it might be the day-to-day user tapped by the CEO for hidden insights. List *all* of them.

Now map these relationships out. Start with your main persona and then indicate who has influence on them by drawing different size circles and connecting them to your main persona. If someone has a lot of influence on your persona, make their circle bigger; if they're more on the fringes but still part of the equation, make it smaller.

Next, map out your main persona's buying process. Ask yourself who's involved in each step and when they enter the process. This includes the main persona(s) and the people who influence them.

Going through this exercise will help you discover the true stakeholders outside of the traditional "chain of command" and how they influence each other. By recognizing this larger group of people and how they operate, you'll be able to identify where you need to devote your time and attention.

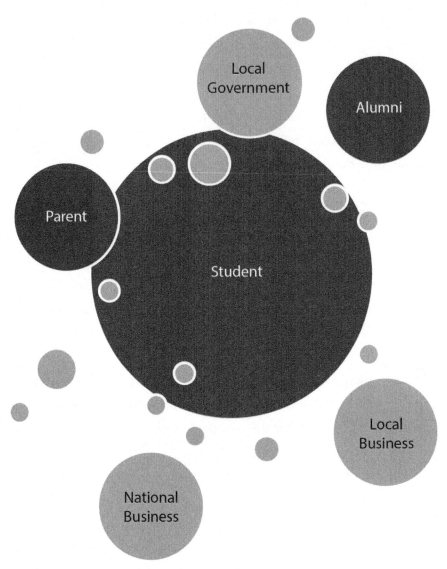

Mapping the relationship between personas illustrates which ones have influence, and how much, with the decision makers.

CREATING AUDIENCE PERSONAS

Meet Jeremy. He's in his mid-30s and loves coffee. He has a great career going in the IT department of a fast-growing bank. Because his days are hectic, it's easier for him to use email; the phone's just another demand for his attention. He's frustrated because his company is growing so fast that it's difficult to keep up.

Jeremy's a family man, and he doesn't want to spend all of his evenings and weekends working. But he's concerned about his career and wants to take advantage of opportunities to grow.

If you were going to give Jeremy a unique value proposition (UVP), what would it be? What matters to him is being effective. If he could be just 25% more effective at work, he'd feel like he was doing a better job of contributing. Plus, he wouldn't be preoccupied with other things when he's home with his family.

Jeremy's UVP is simple: *Give me more time to be me.* Forget about trying to sell him features and benefits—talk to him in a way that makes your company matter to him. This is how you're going to deliver value to him in a way that he cares about. After you have the essence of Jeremy squared away, think about who influences him. Enter influencer persona #1: Cheryl.

Cheryl is the CFO for the bank and signs the checks for the providers that Jeremy picks. While Jeremy worries about being effective, Cheryl is more concerned with saving hundreds of thousands of dollars for the bank. How will you help her do that?

Going one step further, what's the one thing that matters most to Cheryl that doesn't have anything to do with what you sell? Cheryl's personal UVP: *Make me a CFO rock star at my bank.*

You're starting to see the connection, aren't you? Stop and think: Who else in the ecosystem of people you deal with every day do you have an opportunity to influence?

Dig deep into your persona to find out what matters to them most. Put your reporter's hat on and start investigating—start looking for the *real* story. Find out what they're emotionally attached to:

- What does she do?

- What does her day look like? Look into what kinds of frustrations, pressures, and concerns she has. What drives her? What needs does she have that aren't being met?

- Where is the gap in her needs/wants, even beyond your product or service?

- When does she need to close the gap?

- Why does she care about *you*, and not just your product or service?

- How does she connect? Is it online or in person? Is it through white papers, research reports, or demos? Does she use a laptop or her smartphone?

We once had a vice president for a client who traveled for 12 weeks to meet with customers. He wanted to see, hear, and experience firsthand what mattered most to the people his company tried hard to connect with every day.

Here's what he learned: 75% of the things his brand talked about had no relevance to what customers actually wanted. It just wasn't valuable in their world.

But through all of these personal conversations, and by being curious, the vice president discovered something very important. He learned that his company's enterprise training program—a train-the-trainer program—delivered tremendous value to their customers.

This vice president's job all along had been to roll out software products. But once he knew what really mattered to customers, the company began to create a much more robust train-the-trainer program. It was a huge success, but it only happened because he took the time to get to know the brand's customers, and those who influenced them, as people. That's when the company was better able to serve buyers.

JOURNEY + JOURNEYER: BUILDING THE BIGGER PICTURE

As we've discussed, the sales funnel is no longer relevant and brands no longer guide the customer decision journey. Even though customers have access to a great deal of information, that doesn't mean the information they access is relevant in those critical moments when they need to make decisions.

Now more than ever, it's important to understand your personas, their motivations, and the people who influence them. Put the parts and pieces together to build a bigger picture of the journey your customers move along to make a decision and the audience for whom you're trying to create meaningful experiences. How does it all come together? It's different for every brand.

KEY CONCEPTS IN THIS CHAPTER

- People experience a brand in numerous ways, many of which the brand cannot create or control. That is why it's essential for marketers to understand that it's the experience they create that matters most.

- More than 100 years old, the sales funnel is no longer relevant to understanding how to connect with audiences. The customer controls the journey. Your role as a marketer is to take a holistic approach to understanding that journey, and create experiences to accompany it.

- To build deeper relationships with audiences, brands have to create experience-driven touchpoints beyond what they sell. Consider the example of the Michelin Green Guides; their purpose isn't to sell tires, but to help people with their travel plans.

- Understanding and documenting buyer personas is more important than most marketers realize. You won't be able to create relevant experiences for your buyers and those who influence them if you don't have a deep understanding of who they are.

ENDNOTES

43   http://hbr.org/2005/12/marketing-malpractice-the-cause-and-the-cure/ar/1

44   Barry, Thomas. 1987. The Development of the Hierarchy of Effects: An Historical Perspective. Current Issues and Research in Advertising, 251-295.

45   http://advertisinghall.org/members/member_bio.php?memid=692

46   http://www.mckinsey.com/insights/marketing_sales/the_consumer_decision_journey

47   http://blogs.hbr.org/2014/05/marketing-can-no-longer-rely-on-the-funnel/

48   http://www.teslamotors.com/de_AT/forum/forums/tesla-isnt-just-car-or-brand-its-actually-ultimate-mission-mother-all-missions

49   http://www.teslamotors.com/blog/all-our-patent-are-belong-you

50   Interview with Carla Johnson, December 19, 2014.

51   Ibid.

52   Ibid.

53   http://blogs.hbr.org/2014/05/marketing-can-no-longer-rely-on-the-funnel/

54   http://www.viamichelin.com/

55   https://www.siriusdecisions.com/Blog/2013/Jul/Three-Myths-of-the-67-Percent-Statistic.aspx

56   Peterson, Erik and Riesterer, Tim. *Conversations that Win the Complex Sale.* The McGraw-Hill Companies, 2011.

chapter 5:
THE FOUR ARCHETYPES OF CONTENT CREATION MANAGEMENT

"Greatness is not a function of circumstance. Greatness, it turns out, is largely a matter of conscious choice, and discipline." | Jim Collins

How do we evolve from good to great content-driven experiences?

In the first chapter of one of the best business books of all time, *Good to Great*, author Jim Collins starts with a simple sentence, "Good is the enemy of great."[57]

Collins describes what he means by telling the story of a dinner he had with thought leaders. During the meal, one of the participants chided Collins by telling him how much he had enjoyed his first book,

Built to Last, but that the major point was actually quite useless. Collins recounted what his dinner companion said:

> "... *The companies you wrote about were, for the most part, always great. They never had to turn themselves from good companies into great companies. They had parents...who shaped the character of greatness from early on. But what about the vast majority of companies that wake up partway through life and realize that they're good, but not great?*" [58]

This hits home for businesses that are attempting to either modify their existing marketing purposes, or completely upend existing content programs for something that is scalable to create experiences for their customers. With existing silos, processes, and business culture already in place, many marketers are wondering, *"How can we evolve from good to great content marketing within our organization?"*

PURPOSE-DRIVEN CONTENT

Every piece of content a business creates *must have purpose*. Ultimately, that purpose comes down to why and how the content is designed in order to change a behavior in the person who consumes it.

Before we can create a purpose, we must *believe in* what we're saying. However, truth and fact are very different things.

Think about some of your own experiences with marketing. Here are some things we know to be true. We *know* that we're not really going to drag and drop and edit presentations, or work on movies on our iPhone 6. The TV commercial showing people doing that on their iPhones makes it seem like it's easy. All you have to do is tap with your finger, swipe over the graph, and everything will automatically be put into the keynote presentation on your tablet. But no one does that. It's "true"—but, come on, it's not really fact.

We also know that when we have an unfortunate hotel situation, and we get that sympathetic Tweet from the hotel's social media person, that it's simply not a fact that they are "sorry to hear about our problems." It's "true," but the fact is they're actually just trying to get our complaint to disappear from their screen as fast as possible.

We also know, for a fact, that the classic Coca-Cola ad from the 1970s—that taught the world to sing—was completely contrived. That commercial was rehearsed for more than five hours before they shot it. And, yes, we also know that when we go to see *The LEGO Movie* that they're actually trying to get us to buy more LEGOs.

The point with all of this is, *we don't care*. The iPhone 6 commercial is trying to persuade us. The hotel is trying to ameliorate us, the Coca-Cola ad is trying to engage us, and *The LEGO Movie* is trying to entertain us. But we don't care because we're finding value in the experience regardless.

Marketers, we are not in the business of facts. We are in the business of *what ought to be the truth*.

This might be best exemplified with the quote from Blanche DuBois, in *A Streetcar Named Desire,* when she said, *"I don't want realism. I want magic! Yes, magic. I try to give that to people ... I don't tell truths. I tell what ought to be the truth."*

Facts are boring. Facts are commodities. Facts are not differentiating.

CREATING VALUE WITH CONTENT

Year after year, Content Marketing Institute's annual survey shows that "producing enough content" and "producing engaging content" are among the top challenges for B2B and B2C marketers.

But understand that these are just symptoms of a greater challenge. The problem is not the marketer's actual ability to create enough engaging content. The problem is that we are convinced we don't *know how* to create value with content.

This is how it typically goes:

1. We think we don't know how to create valuable content *so...*

2. We don't prioritize the time to create it (if we had a nickel for every time we've heard "content comes after my day job" we'd be rich) *which...*

3. Feeds the perception that we need to create A LOT of it, so that we hedge our bets on the content that will be successful *so....*

4. We outsource it to agencies, freelancers, or people who we *think* "understand content creation" better than we do *which over time produces...*

5. Derivative, unoriginal content that doesn't differentiate our brand or approach at all *which...*

6. Convinces us that our story (or value we could provide) isn't nearly as interesting as we once thought it was *and this...*

7. Brings us back to #1 above.

This needs to change.

CATEGORIZING CONTENT

So, how *do* we create value with content? Well, we can teach with content. We can evangelize with content. We can tell stories that make emotional connections with content. But first we have to know what *type* of content we're creating. Categorizing content by type not only improves our effectiveness, it also helps us know when and where to outsource content production as we scale.

Now, we couldn't resist using a play on the classic four P's as a method of defining content archetypes. If you don't care for these, please develop your own. The point is: do it.

1. THE PROMOTER

Promoter content is the content we're most familiar with. We already create this type of content every day. Examples include our website, brochures, case studies, advertisements, and landing pages. This is the content we create to describe the value of our products and services—and propagate it through all the different channels we manage, including the Internet, mobile, social, television, and print.

Promoter Content
Feeding the needs and wants of audiences

Preacher Content
Feeding discovery and answers for audiences

Professor Content
Feeding the interests and passions of audiences

Poet Content
Feeding the feelings and beliefs of audiences

The four archetypes of content purpose help the team focus on what effect we are trying to have with our content.

Target Attributes of Promoter Content

Promoter content engages our audience's *needs and wants, leading them toward a commitment.* It is structured to persuade—to make an argument in our favor. It may be structured as a story, or as a simple call-to-action. The renowned social scientist Robert Cialdini has done important work involving this kind of content; his book, *Influence: The Psychology of Persuasion,* is one of the seminal works in this space. In a blog post for *Harvard Business Review*, Cialdini discussed attributes of persuasion:

> *"Research shows that persuasion works by appealing to a limited set of deeply rooted human drives and needs, and it does so in predictable ways. Persuasion, in other words, is governed by basic principles that can be taught, learned, and applied."* [59]

Goals of Promoter Content

Put simply, promoter content drives *decision.* It is meant to appeal to the audience and drive commitment to an action. It is content that is designed to get the sale, drive a subscription, initiate a conversation with a sales person—or in some other way persuade the audience to take an action that furthers the business.

2. THE PREACHER

Preacher content evangelizes our remarkable ideas. We develop this content to attract new audiences.

Target Attributes of Preacher Content

Preacher content drives an audience's *discovery and awareness*. Its purpose is merely to be found and promote a larger idea in an easy-to-consume way. Examples of preacher content include "top 5 blog posts," "listicles," or the "weekly newsletter." Or, preacher content can be part of a social strategy that pushes out curated content.

This is the content that has truly exemplified the "inbound marketing" movement, where content's purpose is to "be found." As Brian Halligan and Dharmesh Shah say in their book, *Inbound Marketing: Get Found Using Google, Social Media, and Blogs*:

> "*To make this double win work for your company, you need to create lots of remarkable content. The people who win really big on the web are the media/content companies, who have a factory for creating new content. Each piece of content that has links to it can be found through those sites linking to it and through Google, and it can be spread virally through social media sites.*" [60]

Goals of Preacher Content

The purpose of preacher content is to drive *awareness* and *engagement*. As Halligan and Shah also say in their book, "*the trick is to stand out by becoming remarkable (unique and valuable) to a segment of buyers.*"

3. THE PROFESSOR

One of the key goals of content is to use it to solve customers' problems. One way to do that is to position your company or someone in it as a "thought leader" or (as we prefer) "authority" on a particular topic—and, in that capacity, educate your audience.

Target Attributes of Professor Content

Professor content feeds our audience's *interests and passions*. Examples include any type of content that offers to "help" and "teach," rather than sell, persuade, or make aware. Jay Baer's book, *Youtility*, is one of the most important, and popular, books on this type of content. In it, he says:

- *"If you sell something, you make a customer today. If you help someone you may create a customer for life."*

- *"There are two ways for companies to succeed in this era: be 'amazing' or be useful. The latter is much [more] reliable and viable."*

- *"Youtility is marketing so useful, people would gladly pay for it."*

Goals of Professor Content

The purpose of professor content is to drive *meaning*. It establishes us as an authority within our industry and engenders trust that our expertise will make the customer's life better. This content should be so extremely valuable and unique that it can't be found anywhere else. This means that it will be more carefully crafted than any of the other types of content we produce. It will also, almost assuredly, be sourced in a much different manner.

4. THE POET

This may be the most misunderstood, but most talked about, of all the content types, primarily because it is most often associated with "telling the story" of the business. To be clear, *all* of the content types should contribute to the story of the brand and, more importantly, its approach to creating differentiating experiences for audiences. However, poet content differs from other content types because it helps us connect emotionally. It is the only type of content that can actually *change* a belief.

Target Attributes of Poet Content

Poet content drives *feelings* and *beliefs* in our audience. Examples include any type of content that appeals to the pure emotions of our audience. We are looking to make them laugh, cry, or feel some emotion that aligns with our story or purpose. We are, in essence, bringing them along on a journey—the way any storyteller would. If our goal is to introduce something that will truly change a paradigm of thought, or require a new way to look at things, poet content is truly the only kind of content that has this power.

One of the most interesting examples of this is Coca-Cola's effort to "share happiness." As Jonathan Mildenhall, who was then vice president of global advertising strategy and creative excellence for the company, told Robert Rose in an interview, " ... *[the] more we can fill the emotional well of our audience, we have to trade on it less and less.*"

Filling the emotional wells of our audience is the heart of poet content.

Goals of Poet Content

The purpose of poet content is to drive *emotionality*. Poet content aims to make our audience *feel* differently. It focuses on changing a belief about a particular thing.

HOW THE ARCHETYPES DIFFER

The first thing to make clear is that all of these archetypes have a distinct purpose. The key is to understand the differences, so that when we're creating a purpose-driven piece of content, everyone is on the same page about what *kind* of content we are creating. Let's look at a summary:

ARCHETYPE	DELIVERS VALUE TO THE CUSTOMER BY FEEDING/CHANGING	DRIVES
Preacher	Discovery & Awareness	Engagement
Professor	Interests & Passions	Meaning
Poet	Feelings & Beliefs	Emotionality
Promoter	Needs & Wants	Decision

The desired effect, or purpose, of each archetype of content can help us understand the balance of all the content the marketing teams are creating.

Now you may ask yourself, "Can't every bit of content contain all of these archetypes?" The answer is, theoretically, yes. But, having all of the purposes embedded into the content rarely makes it better, and often ruins it.

Think about the last time you saw a TV commercial clearly advertising the existence of a new product, while it taught you some important lesson in an emotional way. Never seen it? I don't think we have either.

But it's not that it can't be done, and certainly many pieces of great content do blend two or more elements. Here are some of the key differences:

1. **Promoter content** almost always talks about our company, product, or service. This is true marketing and ad copy, plain and simple. One of the most common mistakes that content marketers make is inserting promoter content into professor content and calling that a differentiated experience. Think about that white paper that's really just a case study in disguise.

2. **Preacher content** is often ephemeral. It's commonly topical and created in near real-time. It's also usually part of a high-volume strategy—so it doesn't have the same care and feeding going into it as a deep research piece might. One of the most common mistakes of a nascent content marketing strategy is assuming that all you need is preacher content. If there's no substance behind the evangelizing, you'll quickly run out of parishioners.

3. **Professor content** is, by definition, unique to the brand's approach. It must be high-quality, well-thought-out content. It is the content we invest in—the content that represents our unique approach to the world—and it's often hand-delivered. This content helps us build trust with our customers by showing that we share a similar point of view. A common mistake here is the "nothing to no one" phenomenon. A brand is fearful of taking a distinct point-of-view on a topic, thinking they might disenchant a small segment of a potential audience. Then, by trying to be everything to everyone, they end up being nothing to no one.

4. **Poet content** is also, generally speaking, more sparingly used by most brands. It is meant to change a belief or affect feelings, so it is almost always well considered. It is different than professor content because, ultimately, it is simply intended to create an emotional bond with the audience. It doesn't have to "teach," deliver an "authoritative point of view," or provide any other type of usefulness. It just needs to deliver a compelling emotion that aligns with the brand's point-of-view.

A piece of preacher content can also be a piece of poet content. Your brand might offer up a high-volume Twitter stream with the sole purpose of making people laugh. Or you might argue that the classic Sarah McLachlan commercial imploring us to donate to the ASPCA, while pictures of sick and abused pets are shown, is a mix of promoter and poet content.

The key is not to get so far into classifying each piece of content that putting each piece into an archetypal bucket becomes more important than the goal. The critical thing to understand is the goal for each piece of content and its purpose.

A B2B TECHNOLOGY COMPANY EVOLVES ITS CONTENT PURPOSE

Consider this example of a large B2B software firm in Silicon Valley. This company produces different software across a number of different business functions.

John, a new senior-level enterprise sales representative, was brought on to work at the company because of his expertise in the financial services industry and especially because of his work at large banks. Upon his arrival, John discovered that he would be selling all of the different types of software the company offered. There was certainly no way he was going to be a subject matter expert on each piece of software, but he knew that he'd have access to sales engineers who would help him.

But within days, John found himself overwhelmed with content. Product marketing teams added him to their email lists and soon he was receiving daily emails from each group with content assets attached. Each email would go something like this:

Dear Sales Rep,

Attached please find the latest (infographic/case study/brochure/spec sheet/webinar link/white paper, etc.) for the XYZ product suite. This content represents the latest and most up-to-date thinking in the XYZ space. Please use this content as a key piece with your prospects. You'll also find this content on the HammerNet (their cute name for the marketing/sales intranet).

Thank you for your help with XYZ product suite. Oh, and we've also attached the latest white paper and sales deck slides that you should be using in all of your pitches.

Sincerely,

XYZ Product Marketing Manager

There was only one problem: this exact, same email came daily from seven different product marketing teams and also from an industry-focused consulting group that would send him duplicates (along with their own content that focused on how great they were).

By the end of the first week, John received 500 emails of content covering all of the company's products and services. It was four gigabytes of digital assets every week. He decided to make Monday mornings his day to go through all that content and "learn" about each of the products, so that he could make sense of each piece and file them as "sales content," "thought leadership," "general marketing," etc.

By the end of his first quarter at the business, the email was just too much for him to keep up with. To make matters worse, John was getting regular weekly emails from IT, asking him to prune his inbox as he was going over the storage quota. He began to delete emails on Sundays from the most egregious product marketing teams. John's Monday "learning sessions" quickly dissolved and he prioritized potential client meetings, team meetings, and other things instead of learning.

By the end of his third quarter, John had hacked his own solution to the problem. He noticed that of all the content he received, a fairly large portion of it ended up, final-approved, on the company website. So, when preparing for a potential client pitch or trade show where he would need the latest materials, he simply went to Google and used the command to search the company's site. (He found the company's website search lacking.) Then, he would find and pull those materials, knowing that if they were on the website, he could actually use them. He forwarded those materials to *another* agency, which he had engaged separately for himself and his team. He then asked this agency to create pitch decks and other materials that he would use.

So, all in all, of the four gigabytes of content the product marketing teams were sending him weekly, this enterprise sales rep was using *exactly none of it*.

This company clearly needed to evolve.

Once John's story became more widely known, other sales reps admitted to doing similar things. Some disregarded all of the content, unless it came from product marketing teams that they liked. Some filtered buckets of email to their spam folder and asked product marketing teams for materials only when they needed them. Some only used the HammerNet intranet system as a document repository.

The company decided to create a better way. They developed a content creation and curation process focused on sales enablement. As a first step, this group acted as a filter. They received the onslaught of email from each of the product marketing teams. Their job was to take *all* of this content and repackage it, combine it, reuse it, filter it—basically curate it so that the feed that would go out to both the intranet and by email to the enterprise sales reps contained only the best content.

This group created a training and engagement program in which they would not only send an email, but also create events sharing best practices about the use of certain content in the sales process. They created a feedback loop from the sales reps about which content resonated the best in pitches, which content was hardest to use, that which they didn't understand, and that which was most popular. They created metrics in the intranet as well. With deeper engagement from the reps, they could measure not only what the reps *said* was the most popular content, but identify what content was ACTUALLY the most downloaded. They fed this back to the product marketing teams.

We worked with this team to create a designation and operating model around the creation of content. They discovered that some product marketing teams created *only* promoter content. Some were *very* heavily weighted to professor content (thought leadership) and therefore didn't send much at all. Some were *only* sending high-velocity "blog post"-type material and having a terrible time differentiating.

Using this model helped them improve the way they created and promoted content. For example, when they received a piece of professor content, they would create three preacher content pieces as a promoter for it (as a rule). They weren't offering just a "publishing" or "curation" service, but providing valuable insight into the *purpose* of creating content to begin with.

This ultimately helped them make the case for taking over some of the content creation and design duties. It also provided the product marketing teams with the flexibility to actually produce the "thinking," the "stories," and the material for content, while allowing the creation and curation group to handle the packaging, distribution, and final expression of that content across *all* of the company functions.

A PHARMACEUTICAL COMPANY PUTS CONTENT ARCHETYPES TO WORK

As the software company case above demonstrates, we often must evolve into different content models. In that example, there was an immediate benefit from understanding the type of content being created and how it was used.

But in another case—a pharmaceutical company—the need was to build something from scratch. In this situation, the company was trying to target both customers (from a brand story perspective) and healthcare providers (from a thought leadership perspective). In addition, as a pharmaceutical company, they were under strict compliance and regulatory rules about how and where they could use content.

First, we worked with them to build a Content Creation Management (CCM) process within their brand/corporate communications office (we'll get into more details about this process in the second half of the book); this became their central group. With a complete structure and process in place, the company was able to align its goals with its marketing calendar. However, they still needed to determine who would create what type of content for each audience:

- For brand stories directed toward consumers, they would need "reporters" pulling stories from global regions and then writing them with a "poet's" eye, in order to achieve the emotional brand engagement they wanted to obtain in different regions.

- For professor content directed toward healthcare providers, they would need both in-house subject matter experts as well as writers who knew how to create content for highly specialized areas.

- For promotional advertising about their products, they would need the expertise and feedback from sales teams in each country as well as campaign creation expertise from specific agencies.

- And underpinning all of that, they would need someone who could take some portion of *all* that content and transform it into high-velocity, "snackable" content that could be shared across the brand's social and blog channels.

Ultimately, the company decided to assign teams responsible for content by archetype:

- Promoter content is driven by the marketing and sales enablement teams at the product marketing level. They're responsible for the brochures, ads, and other materials needed to "sell" products in specific regions.

- Preacher content is managed by the web, demand generation, and social teams, which oversee all the content being produced. They repackage it for promotion through social channels.

- Professor content is built by an in-house production team in concert with corporate affairs and subject matter experts.

- Poet content is handled by team members from the overall brand group as well as representatives in each country who share local stories. They work with an agency to bring the stories to life.

In this example, the archetypes gave the company a way to organize the different groups that were creating content. The central group was empowered to manage the balance, the velocity, the budgets, the calendaring, and the creation of new content that moved the business forward.

The detailed methods to create a CCM organization are covered in the second half of this book. But, even if your organization doesn't create a separate governing group, you can benefit by looking at the reasons why you are creating content. What is its purpose? Usually, when you analyze it, you'll see that you are imbalanced in some way. So, you simply need to reorient your business toward a more balanced content marketing and experience-creating strategy. Put the four archetypes to work in your company, and you'll be well on your way.

KEY CONCEPTS IN THIS CHAPTER

- If marketers are to expand the purpose of content to create value, they will be creating content for diverse purposes. Classifying content by using archetypes helps us see how every piece of content fits into the overall marketing and communications strategy.

- As we scale with purpose, we will have different reasons to create content-driven experiences.

  o We will continue to advertise and describe the value of our brand, our product, and our content itself with *promoter content.*

  o We will evangelize and create great quantities of content that make customers aware of our approach with *preacher content.*

  o We will teach our customers and create trust by demonstrating our authority on topics and sharing our knowledge by creating *professor content.*

  o We will create an emotional bond and empathic relationships with our customers through *poet content.*

- Use the four archetypes to help you communicate the different purposes behind the content you're creating; however, don't get so wrapped up in classifying content that you lose sight of the end goal (creating differentiating experiences).

- Even if you're just getting started with content marketing, looking at the various types of content through a purpose-driven lens can help you to determine your balance of content and develop a strategy for moving forward.

ENDNOTES

57   Collins, Jim. *Good to Great: Why Some Companies Make the Leap... And Others Don't*. HarperCollins, 2011.

58   Ibid.

59   https://hbr.org/2001/10/harnessing-the-science-of-persuasion/ar/1

60   Halligan, Brian and Shah, Dharmesh. *Inbound Marketing: Get Found Using Google, Social Media, and Blogs*. Wiley, 2009.

chapter 6:
CONTENT CREATION MANAGEMENT:
A FRAMEWORK FOR CHANGE

"In times of rapid change, experience could be your
worst enemy." | J. Paul Getty

Right around the time businesses could deploy their first CRM systems
(at the beginning of the century), they also started putting in their first
content management systems.

In those days, it was simple. There was one channel, the website, and
everyone focused on how to empower marketing people to publish
digital content easily to the corporate website.

Fifteen years later, it's a different story. The enterprise now manages
innumerable mobile, social, and web platforms. On the day we arrived

for our consultation with a global technology company, they were celebrating the culmination of a six-month process, in which they went from managing 360 campaign microsites to fewer than 50. That's right, they were *happy* to be down to 50 websites.

According to an Association for Information and Image Management (AIIM) study conducted in 2013, more than 80% of companies lacked an enterprise solution to manage content across different channels.[61] However, even a number that big pales in comparison to the percentage of companies that lack a process behind the *creation* of content.

As the enterprise adds more "owned media properties" (e.g., blogs, websites, print magazines, etc.) to its portfolio, the more critical it is to develop a framework to create, manage, and measure these properties. Content Creation Management (CCM) is that framework.

CONTENT CREATION MANAGEMENT DEFINED

Here is our simple definition of CCM:

> *Content Creation Management (CCM) is a conceptual framework to facilitate the organization, creation, development, and management of owned experiential content platforms for marketing purposes. Its goal is to structure an active, functioning and scalable process for marketing departments to create content-driven experiences that differentiate and create value.*

Every organization thinks they know how to create content. But when asked how they do it, most companies can rarely explain the process. Somehow, content just "happens." Very few actually understand CCM as a strategic, repeatable process for creating unique and valuable content.

As we have discovered in our research and interviews with more than 100 companies, both large and small, there currently is no one right way to construct a CCM function within a business. Just as there are myriad ways to structure a newsroom, movie studio, or creative media agency, each company structures the CCM function uniquely for its individual culture and goals.

So, the process of building CCM into your organization will be a journey—one that can, and will, be populated with any number of practitioners within the business. Success will depend on creating a culture that accepts and implements new and innovative best practices.

While undertaking this marketing process journey, the winners will replace the ad hoc "value creation" with *processes that value the quality and execution of ideas.* In fact, CCM is all about *reusing innovative ideas* to continuously improve the company's skill at operating as a media company rather than operating in an endless "campaign creation" mentality, which results in a constant *re-forming* of the idea of "value creation," rinse, and repeat.

In short, the CCM framework transforms content from ad hoc sets of disconnected experiments into a measurable marketing function. CCM is an idea-creation factory—one that manages a portfolio of experience-driven ideas. CCM is a factory expressly built to create a profitable business result. However, its *function* is to create delightful experiences for the customer—through education, entertainment, or general usefulness—pure and simple. It is innovative in nature and built to differentiate the business.

Prior to developing the CCM framework, we studied organizations that are already gaining traction in this area. Some of these companies share commonalities—a finding that suggests a clear way forward. We also pulled best practices from methodologies that center on product development and media management. And we have incorporated ways that media companies operate and manage digital assets. The result is a 12-step framework that is segmented into four main activities that group the steps:

THE 12-STEP CCM FRAMEWORK

1. CREATE CCM
- Inspire a Revolution in the Organization
- Recruit a Team to Lead
- Plan for an Evolution

2. ORGANIZE CCM
- Define Roles and Responsibilities
- Write a Charter for CCM
- Create a Content Mission

3. MANAGE CCM
- Map the Experiences You Will Create
- Build the Experiences and Their Purpose
- Operate a Portfolio of Experiences

4. MEASURE CCM
- Assess the Experiences for Meaning
- Evaluate Stories and Experiences
- Balance the Portfolio of Experiences

① CREATE

Inspire: A revolution in the organization
Recruit: A team to lead
Plan: For an evolution

③ MANAGE

Map: The experiences you will create
Build: The experiences and their purpose
Operate: A portfolio of experiences

② ORGANIZE

Define: Roles and responsibilities
Write: A Charter for CCM
Create: A content mission

④ MEASURE

Assess: The experiences for meaning
Evaluate: Stories and experiences
Balance: The portfolio of experiences

The 12-Step CCM Framework is a process that helps us describe how to manage and measure content-driven experiences within organizations.

Let's look at each of these.

1. CREATE CCM

Content-driven experiences are becoming increasingly important in propelling our businesses forward. But, ironically, we find that the strategy for creating these experiences is rarely driven from the top down. Rather, the earliest glimmer of the process usually has roots deep within the business where a manager is achieving "pockets of success" with a series of ad hoc projects. Eventually, something happens that surfaces that project to full visibility in the organization. In short, that secret little thing off in the corner eventually gets somebody's attention. Then, the inevitable question comes. *"That's the way it's always been done"* is challenged with *"is this the way it should be done?"*

Changing long-held beliefs within an enterprise is, obviously, more difficult in some organizations than others. In some engineering-driven B2B companies, for example, simply getting buy-in to try something that isn't sales-enablement-focused can be a huge task. Yet, fundamentally changing these long-held beliefs is the essential first step. Content practitioners within enterprise organizations must take that early step so that content-driven experiences gain broad acceptance as a viable, successful approach.

So why doesn't this happen more often? Why is it so difficult for people to make this change?

To get insight on this question, we recently talked with innovation expert Thomas Asacker, author of the fantastic book, *The Business of Belief.* He shared a story about meeting with a CEO client with whom he had worked a year earlier. The CEO was lamenting the devastatingly poor results of his company. Asacker asked, "*What did I do wrong the last time I was out there?*" The CEO replied, "*Tom, you didn't do anything wrong. It was great information. But you have to understand, when you left here, everybody had to go back to their jobs.*"

These people understood the change that Tom had suggested and agreed with it. Unfortunately, that understanding didn't drive change. "*That's not what drives action,*" Asacker told us. "*People do what they do because they want to do it. And that's it.*"

In our view, this is just like the classic quote from *The Simpsons* when Homer tells Lisa, "*Oh, honey, just because I understand doesn't mean I care.*"

So what's the answer? How do businesses actually change and create the actions that will drive new approaches such as investing in expensive, differentiating customer experiences? Asacker summed it up well in our conversation when he said:

> "*Where I've seen success is where there's been some outside force—just someone who has figured out how to push a particular leader. It could literally be a brand manager. They lead this leader down, if you will, that bridge of belief, making them comfortable the whole time until they actually release something that's powerful.*
>
> "*The interesting thing is that once they get recognition for actually releasing this creative endeavor, they can then use it as an example for everyone else, saying, 'See, we can do it.'*"

We couldn't agree more with Asacker, as this is how we've seen the process unfold time and time again.

Over the last few years, content marketers have been intensely focused on building a business case and the facts that support their efforts. But, while we need logical arguments for WHY the experiences we create can be justified as investments, we also must INSPIRE people to create those experiences.

The last few years have been focused on how we can actually *build* the intellectual business case to try a content project as a means to engage, help, inform, and change beliefs in customers. But, the next few years should be dedicated to learning how to inspire the company to actually create a strategic, repeatable process to do just that.

So, let's look at each of these major steps in their entirety.

Inspire a Revolution

In almost every case, content marketing, and the idea of creating delightful experiences for customers, starts from a pocket within the business. In a B2B setting, it might be a demand-generation marketer looking to create more value or more leads. Or, it may be a social media person in a consumer packaged goods company looking to feed the social media machine with more valuable, engaging, conversational content. Or, it may be a brand marketer looking to turn the corner on a troubled brand by using a newly constructed story to deliver a novel approach.

Whatever the case, the idea for an organizational approach to CCM rarely starts from the top down. It usually starts with a hunch of inspiration that a practitioner has about improving the world within the business. And from there the idea must either spread up the ladder into corporate branding, sideways into other business units, downward to customer loyalty or other parts of the organization—or all of the above.

And whether this initial idea is one that is fully realized and then used as a prototype to expand the effort, or whether it starts as a more integrated idea that will be spread, it's often done so *without* seeking permission first.

A great example of this is what SAP, a global software corporation, experienced when launching their new customer-experience thought leadership portal, *The Customer Edge*. As Gurdeep Dhillon, global vice president of marketing at SAP, said:

> *"It is very often the case that you need to act first and seek forgiveness, rather than try and build a business case that spends its life in analysis paralysis. We decided that we had two of the three pieces in place needed to execute on a content strategy: the team and a modest budget. So, we set to work addressing the third piece, which for us was a platform upon which we could deliver and measure a customer experience. And once we made that decision, the path to launching the Customer Edge became very clear."* [62]

This initial inspiration is often a disruptive and innovative new approach. It is commonly a highly experimental project that is created to test a hypothesis. Approved or not, an experimental project can be a great way to begin building an organization-wide approach to developing content-driven experiences.

One of the best ways to determine where to build this experiment, or receive the hunch, is to look at the existing funnel and ask, *"Where does it hurt the most?"*

- If the business has an awareness challenge, maybe that's a place to start.

- If the business has no problem drawing leads into the funnel, but fails at nurturing them, maybe that's the place.

- If the business has a challenge in keeping customers loyal, perhaps that's the inspiration.

- If one particular product group, or office, is ready, willing, and able to experiment, start there.

No matter where you begin, know that this seed can spur the business to completely revolutionize what it is doing from a marketing perspective.

Recruit a Team

There is a huge business challenge: Content, and the idea of creating it as a portfolio of customer experiences (as a practice), is both everyone's and no one's job. In many cases, the initial experiment will ultimately fail because longer-term consistency can't be maintained. **The gap between creation of the initial platform and formation of a team to be responsible for it is one of the biggest reasons that content marketing fails in most organizations.**

For example, let's say an initial blog experiment is launched. The expectation is that "volunteers" from other parts of the business will maintain it. The call goes out via a broadcast email saying that "bloggers" or "subject matter experts" are needed. These people will be expected to contribute content and, in many cases, do so in the short term. Then, over the longer haul, life just gets in the way. Content production is not part of their official job description, so these subject matter experts fall short. In most cases, in spite of their best intentions, they just can't justify the time cost of creating content because they have their "day job" to do.

This is one reason that outsourced freelancers are so commonly used by those trying to launch a content marketing or experiential initiative. It's just easier to pay freelancers than it is to cajole internal producers to create the same content.

This is why it is vital to understand and map out your entire framework—and then develop a "long game strategy"—prior to (or at least while) conducting your experiment. In other words, you need to have a plan developed for what happens if this hunch actually works.

Developing an integrated network (or team) that may become a CCM team can be a key to making a longer-term hunch pay off. This might initially be a loose affiliation of siloed departmental leaders, an official "content center of excellence" (CCoE), or a fully functioning content department. But, what really matters from the outset is that you identify the content function so the business will recognize it.

In her seminal report, "Organizing for Content: Models to Incorporate Content Strategy and Content Marketing in the Enterprise," Altimeter analyst Rebecca Lieb sums up the importance of organizing the function:

> *"Organizing for content is both a strategic and tactical undertaking. Businesses that fail to seriously evaluate how and where content fits strategically and operationally within their organizations will suffer in the short term as they strive to continue to create content without cohesion. They will be at a greater disadvantage in the months and years ahead as content demands accelerate in terms of owned content and converged content hybrids in social media and advertising. Orchestrating and fine-tuning content organizationally is the next, most critical step facing marketing."* [63]

The key is to examine the situation and assemble a group that can act formally or informally as the "keepers of content" from a marketing and communications perspective. This may mean a cross-functional group pulled from public relations, brand, customer service, product marketing, digital, etc. (or some subset of those), that builds upon the experiment. And, very quickly, that loose collaboration must be formally recognized.

- FIRST, comes the recognized function by the business leadership;

- THEN, the team forms; it will become the "organization" that tells the story, packages the content, acts as actuary, reuses the content, and aligns content with other marketing functions. In short, it becomes a value-development group to create the valuable product.

Plan an Evolution

Once a team has been identified and/or assembled, the true benefit of the CCM approach comes in seeing how a unified content-driven experience strategy helps drive awareness, increase conversion rates into loyalty programs, and provide for greater customer engagement throughout the lifecycle. It should also create operational efficiencies in terms of the amount of content produced in any given area by different groups.

It's not yet time to formalize this group and plan for the evolution of a CCM process, which can be managed and integrated into the existing marketing function. Rather, we are now starting to assemble a business case for this team to be formally recognized by the organization. The team will ultimately need real power, real investment, and real responsibility.

When building the business case for forming the team, consider including these types of benefits:

- Time savings—a focused team process around content should result in fewer meetings related to content and what to produce.

- Improved velocity of content and integrated ideas, providing for better SEO, richer customer experiences, and more effective use of content across all channels.

- Alignment in measurement across different parts of the buyer's engagement journey.

- Cost savings on content creation that can be fed into more and better content and experience creation.

Many activities must be performed as the plan to formalize the CCM team comes together. These activities will naturally begin to merge into the next phase, which is the design of the CCM. But, resist the initial urge to start designing "formal responsibilities" for the CCM team, and just start "doing"—allowing for talents, capabilities, and desires to emerge. This can be the best way to ensure "buy-in" from a cross-functional team.

The natural evolution of this team will probably look something like this:

- **A steering team**—this team builds the business case and is responsible for getting the C-suite to recognize CCM as an "official" function.

- **An editorial team**—this team makes decisions about budgets, priorities, platforms, and who will manage them; this is the "core team" that will ultimately manage the entire portfolio of experiences.

- **A contributor team**—this team is made up of representatives from various areas that manage and execute the programs developed by the editorial team.

Consider the example of San Francisco's marketing organization, San Francisco Travel. This organization is charged with creating compelling experiences for a diverse set of audiences (e.g., travelers, news media, meeting planners, corporate partners, and influential community stakeholders). They recently developed a centralized approach to creating and managing content-driven experiences.

As Tyler Gosnell, manager of marketing planning and program development for San Francisco Travel, explained:

> *"...We evolved what we were already doing—holding regular editorial meetings in smaller groups—by creating broader and more defined structures and a process that holds members accountable for content delivery and quality assurance. Initially, it was important for us to position our Content Center of Excellence and our new team as merely an extension of processes we already had in place—making it easier to get buy-in and not overwhelming stakeholders. In these early stages, our team has already begun to move immediate needs to get content out the door and toward strategically identifying our content gaps and new opportunities. We feel much more focused and less harried about what needs to be accomplished."* [64]

2. DESIGN CCM

A U.S.-based pharmaceutical and healthcare company with operations in more than 100 countries around the globe designed an innovative content creation management group within the corporate brand department. As a global company, most of their marketing efforts are not only done at the regional level, they are guided by the brand managers for each of the products they produce.

The company's vice president of corporate identity led this charge. He is responsible for the complete brand story for this global company with its huge, diverse range of products.

The company found itself going through a complete rebranding initiative. The goal was to reintroduce itself to customers and to unify businesses that had been recently acquired. The vice president saw an opportunity to create new processes to help tell the company's story more broadly and effectively. In short, he wanted to use customer-centric brand experiences across a number of channels (including web, social, print, and television) to unify the brand story and feed a more holistic company story. His goals were to bring more awareness to other company solutions in nascent markets, such as South America and China, and to provide more brand strength to mature markets, such as Europe and the U.S. With every product group running its own marketing and brand strategy—along with the navigating intricacies, complexities, and regulations of different international markets—this was no small task.

So, what did he do? He built what he called a "content engine" and housed it within the corporate brand group. He appointed a leader of this CCM group, and helped manage and create the organizational process for facilitating the story. The VP then created a charter and a proposed organizational process in which regional offices would (or could) have representation, allowing each to interface with product marketing in its own region. This global CCM group had responsibility for surfacing, curating, creating, packaging, and making available global and locally based stories, which could then be used by local markets. The group was measured on the quality and quantity of stories being consumed by local markets.

One of the keys to launching this was the VP's ability to get the company's new CMO to approve and make this group "official," so that it would be recognized company-wide.

This is a deceptively simple, but vital act—making content and its management for marketing purposes an official and respected part of the process. Failing to do so is the biggest reason why content and experience-driven strategies implode.

Define Roles/Responsibilities

Once you have obtained buy-in (from both senior management and departmental leads) and recognition of CCM as an official function of the business—as well as agreement that experiences are strategic assets worth managing well—you can begin to formalize the group.

Remember Gosnell's point about his experience at San Francisco Travel when he said: *"It was important for us to position our Content Center of Excellence and our new team as merely an extension of processes we already had in place—making it easier to get buy-in and not overwhelming stakeholders."*

In other words, they didn't architect a group and a process in a PowerPoint deck and then seek permission to create it. They created the function and collaboration of a group and went to management with permission to formalize it. This is a crucial difference.

Once you are ready to formalize this group and make it "real" in the organization, you need to take a number of tactical actions. These include, but aren't limited to:

1. Formalizing the roles and responsibilities that managers will have in the CCM process. With some luck, these will be clear from the functions you already established during the "evolution" step, and the members will be eager to accept them.

2. Adding content creation and content management to official job responsibilities and bonus structures.

3. Providing for both accountability and corporate structures for content-centric job functions (e.g., editors, designers, subject matter experts, and reporters).

4. Senior management recognizing that a CCM process and governing body (perhaps called an editorial board or Content Center of Excellence [CCoE] or even content department) now exists—and is not just a virtual team assembled in an ad hoc way.

The structures of a CCM governing body can take a number of forms. These include, but aren't limited to, the following examples:

The Chief Content Officer (CCO)
The department of one

In smaller organizations, this may be the person who is given the charter to create content and experiences with the goal to inform, engage, delight, and differentiate the business. Whether called a CCO, "content strategist," or "content marketing manager," this person is responsible for the development of content and its management as a strategic asset within the business.

The Content Center of Excellence (CCoE)
The cross-functional, "dotted line" team

In larger organizations, it may make sense to create one or multiple CCoE's to facilitate and manage the creation of content in a more holistic, cross-functional way. For example, in a midsized organization, the CCoE may be an assigned cross-functional team that spans public relations, brand, digital, and field marketing—each with content creation and management responsibilities. This group then provides best practices and acts as a governing body to ensure consistency, reuse, and effectiveness of content. In a huge organization, many of these may actually be enabling groups arranged by region, industry group, or other separation.

For example, in 3M (a mammoth organization), Carlos Abler is the leader of online content strategy for global eTransformation. He has created and manages a content-enablement group. His charter is to teach, and ultimately enable, the creation of other CCoEs across 3M. As he sees it, it's not unlike the way a non-profit enables local governments to build successful economies. As Abler said:

"I realized that it was essential to have a framework that could apply to any level of the company, from leadership, to corporate CCoEs, to business service groups, and divisions themselves. The emergence of content champions, and initiatives where pain-points are tightly bound up with the content can and do emerge from anywhere in the company." [65]

The Content Department
The dedicated team

This may actually be the future for most organizations as we enter the seventh era of marketing. Currently, content departments are in-house or even outsourced groups dedicated to creating, curating, managing, packaging, and using content strategically for marketing purposes. In many cases, these groups find homes within more traditional parts of the marketing and communications infrastructure.

Consider how Julie Fleischer, director of content, media, and data for Kraft Foods, leads a dedicated group of content development managers. They create multiple online websites, a print magazine, videos, and social media content supporting a distinct content brand. Fleischer has established a "home" within the media department of Kraft, providing customer research insight and programmatic advertising data services to the product managers, who are responsible for marketing Kraft products.

Authors' Note: Stop here for a moment and reread that last paragraph. Notice how, from a content experiment, Fleischer was able to lean in and build an entirely new business leadership function out of a traditional brand-marketing job, and now has multiple functions as part of her value-creation position. This is the quintessential example of someone who has recrafted her career by focusing on change, inspiring a revolution, and then building an entire dedicated marketing team as a function of value.

Of course, at the other extreme, you'll find companies that have set up their own media operations. For instance, there's Red Bull Media House, a separately run division of the sports drink company. It has been said that Red Bull is really a *"media company that also happens to sell an energy drink."*

The key to all of these models is that others in the business MUST also have content as part of their job function. In the same way that the company accountant has the power to make everyone in the organization responsible for the processes around costs (e.g., filing expense reports, complying with cost policies, purchase orders, etc.), so too must content become a measurable and accountable asset.

Design a Charter for CCM

Whether the CCM governing body stems from the success of an inspirational prototype or is a uniquely created group, once it is ready to start operating, its focus should be on executing against a global editorial strategy.

This strategy will be developed singularly by the team and executed by contributors networked to the group. Or there could be a group that curates the different experiences being managed in other functional areas, serving as a collaborative and communications hub for the company.

Writing a charter for this group will be critical to its ongoing success. Therefore, time should be spent on developing an intelligent set of business goals. The charter can be as straightforward as ensuring that content across the entire buyer's journey (e.g., all customer experience touchpoints) will be delightful, consistent, effective, and measurable. Or perhaps the group will be chartered with creating entirely separate content brands that will support the full continuum of the business, from awareness through loyalty (e.g., the Red Bull model). Multiple groups also could be formed with individual charters that span the gap between different CCoEs (the 3M model).

Independent of the size of the charter, the group's main responsibilities can be wrapped around four main tasks:

- **Planning.** Using long-range calendars to provide budget and executional plans for the types, tone, and categories of content to be created for the business.

- **Storytelling.** Determining, as a group, the overall narrative and experiences that will be created for the brand. What is the company's story (or stories) beyond the products or services it offers? How will these stories be told cross-culturally and cross-functionally in the business?

- **Production and publishing management.** Aligning to global marketing and communications calendars and business goals, this group should be balancing the mechanics of content production against the overall operations of the business. Everything, from new product launches to major corporate events, should be aligned within this group to ensure that stories align to the greater business needs.

- **Engagement and measurement.** This group is ultimately the keeper of the "purpose of content" within the business. It should be tasked with the business case for new platforms, new stories, new content initiatives, and determining how they will be mapped and measured as effective structures within the marketing and communications infrastructure.

Create a Content Mission

Perhaps no other topic gets as much attention as the question, *"What should we talk about?"* Entire books have been written on whether brands should be entertaining, engaging, informative, useful, or all of the above. The one thing that is usually missing is an even more fundamental question, *"What is the purpose of the experience we are trying to create?"*

So, now that the organization has formalized and created a charter, it's time to get busy and start creating. This phase begins to merge into the actual management of the CCM process—and the group will be responsible for either creating new content-driven experiences or improving upon any work that's already begun.

In short, it's time to put content-driven experiences on the agenda.

This is a shift from most marketing strategies. Marketers have been trained to think *medium first* and *content second*. In other words, as marketers, we tend to think, "we need a television campaign" or "we need an email campaign" or "we need a print campaign." And then we backfill with the *message* (or content) that will fill that medium.

Media companies don't do this. When looking to start something new, a media company will begin with the content and the value it will provide to an audience. Then, it will look at how to best deliver that value TO the audience. This is the change we need to make when developing our content mission. We should think *story (or experience) first* and *then* consider the medium through which it will be expressed.

Any business that's looking to create an experience-driven mission needs to ask four simple questions:

1. What is our goal for this experience (what business goal will it satisfy)?

2. Who will satisfy that goal (who is our audience for this new experience)?

3. What value (separate from our product/service) will we deliver to this audience?

4. What makes our approach to delivering this value different?

Let's say our business makes pet food. Here's how we would move through the questions:

- **What is our goal?** A perfectly adequate answer might be "to build greater awareness of our new product."

- **Who will satisfy that goal? What audience?** There is almost assuredly more than one answer here but pick ONE. For example: "the new 'mom' (i.e., owner) of a puppy that has been adopted by the family."

- **What value (separate from our product/service) will we deliver to the new mom?** The answer, in this case, might be education about all of the things that puppies should and shouldn't eat.

- **What makes our approach to delivering this value different?** We'll discuss in Chapter 7 how to get to core values. The key is NOT to stop at "value," but to get to the core differentiator of the business's approach. Perhaps, in this case, it's our brand's belief that puppies should be on specific nutritional diets at specific ages, and that there is a regimen for food that goes way beyond what most pet stores advise.

As our colleague, Joe Pulizzi, says, "*...the content mission is not about what you sell ...it's what you stand for. This will become the basis for your content marketing strategy. It's based on the informational needs of your customers and prospects, and also inherently drives your business.*"[66]

You will ultimately have multiple content missions that support different audiences or different parts of the customer journey. The content mission is truly the center of gravity for EACH of the content platforms that the CCM team will create as part of a portfolio of experiences.

3. MANAGE CCM

Aristotle famously said, *"Well begun is half done."* And, reaching the "manage" portion of our CCM wheel marks the exact halfway point for the CCM framework. The irony is that at this stage many businesses actually start their content-driven experience. In so many cases these days, the strategy is defined by trying to manage the content into some desired (or new) channel.

In other words, a new social channel like Facebook appears, and the business decides that it needs a Facebook strategy and/or team. Or, mobile technologies become the way that our customers want to engage with content, so the strategy question becomes "how do we transform all the content we're doing into a mobile interface?"

As we've discussed, these are simply the wrong questions. In order for any enterprise to scale the number of content-driven experiences it ultimately manages, it will need to understand "why" and "what" content should exist in the first place. And then, it will need to understand "how" it can use, reuse, package, repackage, and manage content on ANY channel that may be developed. If the creation and design of CCM enables the business to have a good handle on "why" and "what," managing CCM will provide it with the means to make smart decisions on "how" and "where" the content will go.

Developing a process to manage the creation and management of individual "owned media" efforts is probably the most critical piece of what a CCM management process is meant to achieve.

The CCM team will, of course, have the charter to manage existing owned content-driven experiences such as blogs, websites, print magazines, etc. But the additional responsibility will be to acquire and/or build new ones as well. That first inspirational "experiment" may or may not be performing well, and it may need a new purpose and editorial strategy. Or, the group may decide that there is an opportunity to purchase an existing and already operational independent property, such as a blog or magazine, which will need to be integrated. Or, this group will need to devise new initiatives that will fit into a balanced portfolio of content-driven experiences. This is where mapping and building stories into a balanced portfolio becomes an important and critical skill for the team.

Keep in mind that there will be multiple "flavors" across initiatives. For example, SAP's Customer Edge blog is a platform that was conceived internally, built with the help of agencies, and is now managed almost entirely by Gurdeep Dhillon's content marketing team. In contrast, American Express leaned more toward outsourcing for its OPEN Network, the educational community for business owners looking for expert advice on managing their companies.

Mary Ann Fitzmaurice Reilly, senior vice president, American Express OPEN, described the model in a July 2010 interview with *Fast Company*:

> *"...it takes a small army, both internal and external," offered Mary Ann, who mentioned a litany of external partners who help with site development, article content, online media, and related live events. When discussing why AmEx sought outside help like Federated Media for bloggers, Mary Ann pointed out that, "You can't do it alone; there are a lot of experts—leverage them to make the most robust solution you can."* [67]

Determining the right model to build and manage a sustainable owned media property will take the collective CCM team's efforts. Time and again, the CCM governing body will be called upon to provide the business case for why a new content platform (e.g., a blog, event, print magazine) will provide value. But then, once the group approves that effort, the management process will be critical to executing the initiative successfully.

Map the Experiences You Will Create

The first step in determining whether any initiative is worth doing (or worth continuing) is to create an executional map, both from an editorial and a project-mapping perspective. The goal of this process is to create a high-level editorial and creative strategy—as well as to define the business goals and measurement—that will justify the existence of a given platform.

Put in its simplest terms, once an initiative has gone beyond the "*this seems like a good idea*" stage, the group has to determine what it will take to make it real.

To accomplish this, we have seen methodologies such as Agile take hold within businesses (especially within marketing groups) and pay some of the biggest dividends for this kind of work. Other methodologies (e.g., the Lean Startup by Eric Ries, Radical Management by Stephen Denning, and Discovery Driven Growth by Rita Gunther McGrath) have created tremendous opportunities and we encourage a deeper exploration of all of these approaches.

But, in Chapter 7, we will take a deep dive into the specific approach that WE recommend for creating a story map for individual initiatives. This very specific methodology is both a template and an operational model to reach two distinct goals. The first goal of the story mapping process is to create an editorial and creative strategy that helps to align the larger story with the brand approach.

Ultimately, the story map not only helps to align business goals, it helps to align the purpose of the editorial and creative to create a compelling experience. Unlike a marketing campaign, the team is building a plan for something that is meant to last. In short, both goals are how to plan the first modules of a permanent space station, not a mission to temporarily orbit the earth and successfully land.

Build the Experiences and Their Purpose

One of the biggest complaints in creating content-driven experiences is that "we have to wait for results." This isn't true. Deploying a smart map—and a process for managing your progress—should give you immediate indication of how you're progressing toward a goal and the ability to course-correct along the way.

Once you have a plan in place, the CCM group may be responsible for managing the ongoing development and execution of your platforms. Referring to the goals and timelines that you established within the initial mapping process will give the team a projection of what "success" should look like at this relative point in time. Then, in order to achieve "success," the CCM team will need to look to "where we are," and then make assumptions about "what needs to be true" at various waypoints along the path.

But, how will you know if you are tracking successfully? What will be the primary indicators of whether this initiative should remain a piece of your experience portfolio? This is the process of "building stories."

As part of Chapter 7, we provide an actionable plan that provides the best chance of success for an innovative, new, and usually unproven customer experience platform. This includes things like project plans, timelines, budgets, success metrics, resources, and all of the other things that will be needed to create and, more importantly, sustain value over the long haul.

Manage a Portfolio of Experiences

Assuming we've established and met our minimally accepted success—and our new experiential or content-driven platform is officially a "going concern"—it's time to make new maps, as well as set the course for ongoing operations of the platform.

Here, more than specific steps, it's important for the CCM process and governing group to infuse a number of core competencies and build processes to support them. These include:

- **Portfolio management.** As mentioned above, the CCM's true mission is to manage the portfolio of experiences related to communications for the business (or perhaps just their part of the business). The strategic management of content as a portfolio of owned, earned, and paid strategies will be the overriding mission of the group. This is where becoming a media company, and not simply acting like one, is so important. The CCM group must manage the entire universe of the content value.

- **Continual innovation.** An eye will be needed to continually look for new story maps and innovations over time.

- **Discipline.** The discipline to manage the portfolio against a larger performance goal (and perhaps an even broader story map) will be critical.

As we explain in Chapter 7, success may simply be about executing exactly as planned. Or, as is most often the case, it may mean improvising based on a sudden, unplanned challenge or obstacle. One of the subjects that we detail in Chapter 7 is how to get into a review cycle that is not based on major developmental milestones, but on progress toward the different phases of the story as the team has mapped it. Exactly how granular you make these rhythmic review cycles will depend largely on how confident you are about the assumptions you've made.

4. MEASURE CCM

At the Content Marketing Institute's Executive Forum in May 2014, the tension around the subjects of measurement and delighting audiences with content was palpable—so much so, that "inventing new forms and paradigms of measurement" was the winning "big idea" of the forum's idea "competition." The consensus that the 50 executive-level participants (from brands of all sizes) reached was that measurement in marketing is fundamentally broken and there should be new ideas proposed to reinvent the way that companies measure success—especially as it pertains to content-driven experiences.

To be clear, this is not a book about marketing measurement. There are innumerable experts in the field who can explain how deriving customer insight out of the mountains of data we are collecting can be transformed into smart business strategies.

However, as it pertains to the CCM process, measurement—especially where it relates to content-driven experiences—needs to be rebooted. The perception of the inability to measure (as opposed to the actual results) is the most often cited reason why content marketing initiatives are cancelled. And so, as we move into the new era of experiences, it will be incumbent upon us as we "lean in with our capital M" to CHANGE how we approach measurement.

Construct Your Measurement Plan

As the CCM team matures and begins to manage more initiatives as part of a portfolio of experiences, it will need to balance the goals of each of these initiatives against the overall performance of marketing more broadly.

In other words, the lead generation experiences may be working beautifully, but perhaps they are affecting (perhaps even hampering) the performance or attention being paid to experiences at the nurturing or loyalty level. This is where creating a measurement plan that fits across the entirety of the portfolio is important.

Discrete groups such as marketing, advertising, sales enablement, PR, and customer service will be doing things that are (hopefully) in concert with what the CCM group is managing. But, many times, resources will need to be rebalanced, or focused on a particular need. A key pillar of CCM is to manage the entire universe of the experience value, not just any one platform.

Think of how George Lucas (and now Disney) manages the portfolio of the Star Wars universe. It's a portfolio of story maps and platforms from movies, to books, to television shows, to products, etc. They all have different heroes, investments, and management teams. They all have schedules and calendars and have to introduce stories in a very particular and logical order. They all have business goals, budgets, revenue to account for, and costs to manage. And, most importantly, they all have overlapping audiences who will know if the "order of the universe" is mismanaged. Everything within that universe conforms to a set of "story physics." How each story map fits into the larger picture is an incredibly important piece of managing the puzzle.

In addition to managing similar responsibilities, your CCM group will be responsible for identifying new story maps and innovating over time. So not only will your team be constantly executing, but also constantly evolving.

In Chapter 10, we propose a complete framework for measuring content-driven experiences and show you how the measurement of these initiatives can be aligned into a holistic dashboard that can be managed by the CCM group.

Evaluate Stories and Experiences

This is probably the most difficult part of creating a formalized CCM function in any business. For many organizations, this kind of radical shift in the way initiatives are pitched, created, managed, launched, and either continued or decommissioned is a fundamental (even emotionally disruptive) cultural shift.

We've discovered that one of the worst ways to make this shift happen is, paradoxically, to take traditional project management practices and segment teams to a "skunk works" type of project. The challenge with this type of approach is that, whether successful or not, the project teams can often have a difficult time integrating themselves into the larger organization. This makes evaluating the value of these types of experiences over time very difficult, because it becomes about the skunk works team fighting for survival rather than the experience being managed.

For example, in one large software company, the marketing organization decided that a "dream team" would be assembled and separated to handle all digital content platforms. Their first project was to create a completely self-driven blog network to make the disparate product groups more "social" and "experiential." Given a mandate by the C-suite, the dream team found themselves using that mandate as a very large stick to "persuade" other members of the existing web, content, social, and marketing teams to change their ways to accommodate the project. Decisions were made solely by the dream team and then relayed down to the various constituents who would have to execute them. As you might expect, politics reared its ugly head, distrust was sown, and ultimately, even though the team succeeded in launching the blog network, the initiative failed. Because no one wanted to continue on with the team, they ultimately lost momentum and the "dream team" was disbanded.

We see this kind of mistake made all the time. A group gets together in a back room and starts making decisions about better processes, new projects, innovations—all on their own.

In contrast, story mapping and the successful execution of a formalized CCM process are almost always about mobilizing the unique strengths and talents of ALL the people in the organization. Therefore, the CCM governing body needs to be inclusive and create self-organizing teams that, in many cases, are external to the governing body. Projects (and story maps) should be created collaboratively, perhaps in replicated workshops that include all manner of teams from cross-functional departments.

As Stephen Denning says in his book, *The Leader's Guide to Radical Management: Reinventing the Workplace for the 21st Century*:

> *"Radical management is about mobilizing the energies, spirit, and ingenuities of workers and focusing them on delighting clients and to go on doing it time after time in a sustainable way. To accomplish that, managers have to abandon their faith in backroom engineering and enlist the workers in taking responsibility for co-creating a new, more productive, and more fulfilling future."* [68]

The ultimate benefit of this approach is the ability to measure and evaluate *experiences*—not the teams creating them. It provides the incentive for teams to work together to optimize the experiences across all channels, and to actually work together to repackage, reuse, and redistribute content and data for common goals rather than siloed goals.

Balance the Portfolio of Experiences

Every investor needs to perform regular portfolio rebalancing. Some of the company's investments in content-driven experiences will be big gainers, some will be moderate successes, and some will fall flat on their faces.

This periodic content rebalancing is a critical piece of moving back into the inspiration phase—with a concerted effort to have low, medium, and high-risk elements in the experience portfolio. This risk doesn't always equate to the simple cost of the project. Your team will almost assuredly develop expensive, but low-risk platforms, and inexpensive but high-risk initiatives.

Jonathan Mildenhall, former vice president of global advertising strategy at Coca-Cola, explained that the company used a 70/20/10 investment strategy to manage its content portfolio. When he sat down with Robert Rose in November 2012, the two discussed how 70% of the budget goes to content that they "must produce," 20% goes to content that is "slightly out of the box," and 10% goes to "high risk" creative content. Rose then asked him if that 10% number translates to a dollar figure as well. Mildenhall responded that it didn't:

> *"Actually it's quite the opposite. It's much cheaper to produce the 10%. But, it takes much more creative time to actually come up with. This is where I, admittedly, have a bit of an advantage. The Coca-Cola brand is one that any number of other brands has a desire*

to align themselves with—from other consumer brands to technology providers who want to innovate and explore new frontiers.

"We are increasingly open to these ideas. If you think about it, Coca-Cola can be viewed as a huge media brand with amazing reach and frequency. If there are pitches out there from people who want to provide content and experiences, we are open to hearing from them. The question we ask ourselves is, 'Can we use our assets as content, and can we create content out of our assets?'"

Ultimately, the goal here is clear: **We want to wrap back around into new ways to innovate and be inspired to create new customer experiences.**

Consider the case of a fictitious $25 million mid-market software company that's managing a number of content-driven experiences:

- A high-level awareness blog—designed to educate customers and convey the brand's point-of-view.

- A thought leadership program—made up of webinars, email nurturing, and a white paper program designed to teach customers best-in-class practices.

- A customer engagement community—made up of customers and out-of-the-box third-party thought leaders who share how they've used the software in innovative ways.

- An influencer program—encompassing physical events, eBooks, and beautifully designed snail mail pieces meant to communicate the "future" to the executives of the companies that use the software.

For this software company, four major initiatives in the portfolio are being managed by the CCM group. Other "experiences" likely make up the promotion of these programs—such as a social media program that promotes both the blog and the thought leadership initiative. The sales enablement plan is likely linked to the thought leadership program and the customer engagement community, if not the influencer program as well.

One cross-functional group (rather than many) is better equipped to examine how content can be leveraged across these platforms. Each platform will also have its own story maps, goals, costs, and success rates. All the platforms are related, and each can be duplicated to create scale across a larger organization.

As one experience initiative grows, the CCM team must ensure that other initiatives can benefit from that growth. As one initiative begins to fail, the group must rebalance the investment in others, either to save it or so that the CCM team can mitigate the risk to the others.

In very large organizations, there may be multiple CCM teams managing multiple portfolios. Some will be well advanced and some will be in their formative "team" assembly. Remember our earlier discussion about Carlos Abler from 3M? He manages a portfolio of CCoEs in varying degrees of maturity. As he told us:

> *"I realized that organizational patterns link up in very interesting ways. One is in the Content Center of Excellence, which we are thankfully seeing more of now. I am also seeing and fostering what I internally refer to as a 'Matrix of Excellence,' or MoE. Various kinds of content initiatives may be managed cross-departmentally and cross-divisionally. This kind of aligned effort is still a type of*

organization, but not a 'center' in the usual sense because they are composed of people with different lines of reporting, geographies, P&Ls and so forth.

"This is inevitable in organizations that have legacy organizational structures based on products or sub-brands and not markets or customers. Additionally, champions can emerge from many disparate role types, from subsidiary marketing director roles to marcoms, segment marketers, or corporate executives. That said, we are also spawning centers in the more traditional sense. My belief is that over time these MoEs will evolve into centers as the organization naturally matures into a more market- and customer-aligned organization, which strengthens and is strengthened by content marketing and agile marketing in general." [69]

Now that we've explored the process, we have to develop our audience. Let's get to work.

WHAT'S NEXT: THE 90-DAY VISION

- The First Month

    o Determine your next step. Do you have a content challenge, or an organizational challenge? You may have a great "pocket of success" that is worth expanding, or you may need to think about how you're going to inspire belief. Put a plan together for how you can make a change.

    o Recruit and assemble a team that can serve as the CCM leadership. Inspire participation first, before formalizing the group. Collaborate to understand how content might be applied at a more holistic level across these groups.

- o Formalize this group with a charter and make the roles and responsibilities clear with management. Change job descriptions; make the business case for content as a function, not a project.

- o Begin to create the first (or a modified) content mission for an existing or new platform.

- The Second Month

  - o Lay-out and story map a number of experiences. Collaborate on how they will benefit each cross-function and assemble the plan for them.

  - o Prioritize and make decisions about which initiatives will make sense, given current budgets and priorities. Develop a plan for the rollout of these initiatives and how they will be measured.

- The Third Month

  - o Start building out the story maps.

  - o Refine the structure of the CCM group. Finalize job descriptions, roles, responsibilities, collaboration on editorial calendars, etc.

ENDNOTES

61 http://techwhirl.com/aiim-study-82-percent-of-companies-lack-enterprise-content-management/

62 Interview with Robert Rose, July 2014.

63 http://www.slideshare.net/Altimeter/organizing-for-content-models-to-incorporate-content-strategy-and-content-marketing-in-the-enterprise-19795236

64 Interview with Robert Rose, July 2014.

65 Ibid.

66 http://contentmarketinginstitute.com/2012/10/content-marketing-mission-statement-2/

67 Neisser, Drew. "What American Express's OPEN can teach us about social media" *Fast Company*. July 12, 2010. http://www.fastcompany.com/1669407/what-american-expresss-open-can-teach-us-about-social-media

68 Denning, Stephen. *The Leader's Guide to Radical Management: Reinventing the Workplace for the 21st Century*. John Wiley & Sons, Inc., 2010.

69 Interview with Robert Rose, July 2014.

chapter 7:
STORY MAPPING: MANAGING THE CREATION OF EXPERIENCES

"If you want a happy ending, that depends, of course, on where you stop your story." | Orson Welles

In our experience, there is no shortage of innovative ideas within companies. However, a huge wealth of ideas never gets a chance to be expressed.

Leadership in companies often talks the talk of innovation, but rarely walks the walk. A great example of this comes from the world of PR agencies. We all know that for the last 10 years, the PR agency business has been under a fundamental disruption. One senior manager in one of the largest PR agencies in the world recently told us:

"We often have all-hands meetings where senior management gives a very inspirational speech, about how we must be innovative and deliver new content marketing, and strategic social media solutions to our clients. And then, once the speech is over, we all go back to our cubes and try to get reporters on the phone to get coverage for our clients."

Companies want their marketers to be innovative—you know, as long as they can prove ROI on that innovative new thing they want to try.

Innovation just isn't built into the DNA of most larger companies these days. Most middle managers make senior manager by simply operating more efficiently than others in the organization. They sell incrementally more, they convert incrementally better, they hire incrementally better agencies, and achieve incrementally better financial results. This takes absolute discipline and focus, no doubt. But it does not lend itself to a culture of innovation.

As Peter Drucker said back in 1985 in his classic article, "The Discipline of Innovation":

"Innovation is the specific function of entrepreneurship, whether in an existing business, a public service institution or a new venture...

"Most innovations, especially the successful ones, result from a conscious, purposeful search for innovation opportunities, which are found only in a few situations."

Every innovative initiative starts with an idea and content-driven experiences are no exception. Whether they are driven by a member of the social media team looking to make a social channel more relevant, or by the demand-generation team seeking to make B2B sales processes more efficient, or maybe even the public relations team looking to create a more compelling corporate brand story—the idea is a seed that either gets germinated or squashed.

As we discussed in Chapter 6, part of the role of the CCM group is to provide both a forum and an incubator for these ideas. But simply brainstorming, while fun and often *very* productive, often leads to a list of great ideas that end up abandoned for a host of reasons.

Typically, innovative experience ideas are killed because of excuses such as "that's not how we do things" or "that will never get sales support." Other reasons include:

- They seem too complex.

- Buy-in was never obtained from the executive suite.

- The ideas made it to the execution stage, but never met estimated measurement goals, so they were dropped a year later.

- Truly innovative ideas are stuck in small sandboxes. Far too often, a completely transformative idea is trapped inside a single white paper because that's how it was first conceived.

To make the creation of content-driven experiences a scalable and manageable process, we need a structure for creating and mapping ideas—along with a way to estimate the value of those ideas among the projects being considered. Story mapping is a great way to create that structure.

WHY CALL IT STORY MAPPING?

The term *story mapping* is used in a number of past and current contexts. It is most predominant as a component of Agile software development, where it refers to the idea of grouping user "behaviors" (or stories) as a workflow to describe how software should behave. This is, in turn, a byproduct of the "Extreme Programming" movement in the late 1990s, which employed user stories (or use cases) as a way to develop products.

Today, the practice of story mapping in software development enables architects to arrange the user "stories" into models that help them understand how the broader functionality of a larger software product should be developed. It helps establish a context for the developers to identify gaps or omissions in the development—and more effectively plan for larger releases or versions of the product.

Additionally, story mapping is a term used by those in the creative narrative space. From screenwriters to playwrights to novelists, the term is used to describe how to effectively map (usually in some graphical template or outline form) the key elements of the story's characters, setting, conflict, major plot points, and resolution development.

In our approach to mapping content-driven experiences, we're using the spirit of both the software and narrative contexts to create a high-level story structure. For us, the story map and the story mapping process enable a CCM-focused team to add a structural form to a larger creative idea about engaging a specific audience.

As we've said before, CCM is an ongoing process. In order to sustain this managed process, as well as to scale it as a functional piece of the business, each initiative (just like every product development) needs a structure, a purpose, and (perhaps most of all) a way to measure the value created.

In short, the marketing organization (or the CCM governing body within it) starts to operate not *like* a media company—but *as* a media company. It manages a portfolio of one- or multiple-owned experiential platforms that create value for audiences. The CCM story mapping process is a method to create the clear structure and to define the experiences that make up the portfolio.

Parts of our story mapping process will be familiar territory to those who follow Agile methodologies, the work of Eric Ries and his Lean Startup approach, or the work of Rita Gunther McGrath and the Discovery Driven Growth idea. We also borrow heavily from some of the story development and structure best practices presented in Christopher Vogler's book, *The Writer's Journey: Mythic Structure for Writers*. Vogler's book is, in turn, a reinterpretation of the famous work, *The Hero with a Thousand Faces,* by mythologist Joseph Campbell.

Of course, we've also adopted many successful and sticky "best practices" that we've observed while conducting research on brands and working with hundreds of large companies in our consulting engagements.

THE GUIDING PRINCIPLES OF STORY MAPPING

Story mapping has three distinct parts:

1. THE WHY (we always start with WHY)—Our content mission. We begin with a content mission that provides the creative editorial heart, which helps to align the larger story of our brand with this specific initiative. Put simply: This is the value we will

deliver to our audience. Additionally, we define who will receive this value—and why they will care. Finally, we determine how this experience will be different than what is generally available out in the marketplace of ideas.

2. THE WHAT—Our business mission. This starts with our business goal, which answers the questions, *"What does success look like? When should it be achieved?"* We'll discuss this further in Chapter 10, but this is where we differentiate the success of the initiative from its contribution to the business. We also define how the initiative will integrate into other parts of the business, and how it will serve cross-functionally.

3. THE HOW—Our proposed map. The map illustrates how we will approach the initiative over time. Here, unlike outlining a campaign, we are planning for product development. In short, we are planning the first modules of a permanent space station, not a mission to orbit the Earth and come home.

We then bring into this map our purpose-driven content strategy to determine how we will creatively tell our stories over time. We ask ourselves what kind of content balance between the four archetypes we will need:

- How much promoter content will we need to promote this new initiative—and over what time period?

- How will preacher content fit? Will we use it to evangelize this new idea or infuse it into the platform, or both?

- Will we need professor content (thought leadership or how-to content) at this point? Maybe not.

- Will we need poet content to bond emotionally to our audience? Or, will this be purely educational?

- Or, most importantly, how will each type of purpose-driven content play a role in the success of the initiative?

Then, by taking the next three key ingredients in order, we can develop a clear proposal for an initiative so that our CCM Team can make a sound business decision on how to implement and manage it as a key piece of the portfolio of experiences.

The outline of this proposal might look like this:

1. **The Content Experience Mission, with three distinct parts**

   - What is the valuable experience, separate from our product or service, that we can deliver? At what stage of the audience's journey with our brand?

   - Who is this value for? What is the audience persona we are trying to reach?

   - What makes OUR approach to delivering this value unique?

2. **The Business Goals, with three distinct parts**

- What does success of the initiative look like? How will it contribute to the business? Does the initiative have more than one business goal?

- What are the business goals? How long will it take for each goal to be met?

- How will the initiative integrate into the overall business strategy (marketing, sales, customer service, PR, etc.)?

3. **The Story Map, a phased rollout over time**

- Narrative outline—How will the elements of the story be introduced over time?

- Business goal phases—How will we demonstrate progress toward both the success of the initiative and its potential for meeting the business goal(s)?

- Purpose-driven content—How will the balance of content needs change over time?

- Channel strategy—How will different channels be used over time? Where will integration into existing content channels be required?

A FRAMEWORK, NOT A TEMPLATE

The critical idea to understand is that this is a framework, not a template. Some of these initiatives may be more relevant than others. Or, other content platforms may be introduced during different parts of the story mapping process.

For example, the business may decide that instead of *building* an owned media platform (such as a blog or print magazine), it makes more sense to actually buy an existing publication that already has a built-in audience. Or, there may be a merger in which two companies suddenly find themselves managing one or more existing platforms. Or, there may be an existing platform or effort that exists, and the task for the CCM group is to create a "reason" for it to exist.

In all these cases, many of the ingredients listed above can be an important factor in determining the ongoing viability and/or operating model for the platform. In short, it can be useful to go through all the steps, even though a new platform is not necessarily being created.

Additionally, if the new project is quite large (as we'll cover later), there may be a reason to try a "pilot" to test some of the initial assumptions prior to investing in a full-blown project. Conversely, not every project needs to go through such a stringent process. If the effort is small, or is designed to be temporal or seasonal, many of these ingredients can be skipped and/or truncated.

The benefit of the story mapping process is its ability to communicate and represent an experience *before* it is actually developed. Its ultimate purpose may be to serve as the business case or "project vision" for a company. A great story map can be an effective way to make sure that every function in the business is represented and that everyone buys into the vision of what the experience will deliver.

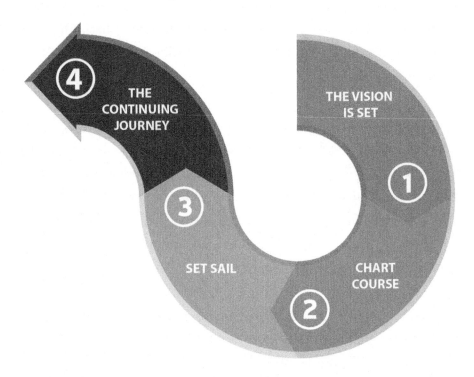

Set the Vision — The "Why" and "Who"
The "content mission": the value created and to whom it will be delivered

Set the Objective — The "What" and "Where"
The executional map of how we will get there

Set the Map — A Product Not a Project
An operating model that enables us to overcome tests and challenges

Sustainability
Becoming part of our portfolio of experiences

The story mapping process helps to organize content-driven experiences into a clear way to communicate the plan of making them a reality and manage them responsibly as a product vs. a campaign.

STORY MAPPING – THE PROCESS

STEP 1: SET THE VISION

As mentioned, there are three ultimate outputs to our story map: the high-level vision of the value that will be delivered (the *why* and the *who*); the actual business goal, integration, and implementation strategy of the idea (the *what*); and the responsible management over time (the *how* we will achieve the vision).

So, if we start with an idea, one of the first things we'll do is determine whether it's a good idea, and whether it's truly valuable to the audience we're trying to reach at that stage in their journey with the brand. To put it into different terms: What we're trying to figure out here is the best *story*, and then determine whether that story is best told as a campfire story, a novel, a television show, a movie, or a series of movies.

Start with Why

Why is at the heart of the story we are trying to tell. It can help us uncover a great idea or expose a mediocre one. But how do we transform what might be a good idea into something that is uniquely valuable to our audience?

One really great method to getting to this overarching story—or core value—is to go through an exercise called the "5 Whys."

The 5 Whys is a process developed by Sakichi Toyoda. It was originally used within Toyota Motors during the evolution of its (now) famous Toyota Production System. It has since been borrowed to be part of the Lean Startup and Agile methodologies. The process is simple: you state a problem, and then probe the "why" question five times (or thereabouts) until you get to the "root cause" of the problem. For each "why" asked, basically the answer is repeated as the question. Here's an example.

Problem: The living room is dark. We can't see.

The 5 Whys:

1. Why is it dark? Because the light bulbs are not working.

2. Why are they not working? Because the light bulbs are dead and burned out.

3. Why are they dead and burned out? Because the light bulbs are old and should have been replaced.

4. Why have they not been replaced? Because we didn't know they needed to be replaced.

5. Why did we not know they needed to be replaced (root cause)? Because we don't have a way to track how old the light bulbs are.

In this case, the root cause is NOT that the light bulbs are not working. That's simply a symptom. The core issue is that we don't have a method to track the age of the light bulbs. Therefore, we can't predict when they will go out, or fix the greater problem, which is a dark room. Unless we get to the core, we will have to fix this problem again. So, fix the root cause and you can more effectively avoid the eventual problem in the future.

There are extensions to the 5 Whys. And, certainly its weaknesses are well documented. But from the perspective of getting to the core aspect of our story from a base idea, asking "why" five (or more) times can be very beneficial.

For example, here are the ideas that most people come up with when asked to create an idea that will work as a content-driven experience initiative:

- Launch a blog that informs users on how to use the kind of product we sell.

- Create a white paper series on the business benefits of the kind of service we provide.

- Use a blog platform to curate news from our industry to position ourselves as thought leaders.

- Create a branded content video that shows a funny actor doing silly things with our product.

All of these *might be* innovative ideas to create a powerful customer experience. But let's take one of these, the "curate news" idea, as an example and run it through our "whys" to get to the true purpose of that idea and how (if at all) it fits into our larger story. *(Note: this example is purposely generic to make the point. We're confident that you and your team will be much more creative here.)*

Idea: Use a blog platform to curate news from our industry to position us as thought leaders.

Target Audience Persona: Our busy CIO customer.

The 5 Whys:

1. Why is curating news to position us as thought leaders important to the CIO?

    Because our CIO customer will see that we have our fingers on the pulse of our business and have a point-of-view on the industry.

2. Why is it important that our CIO customer see that we have our fingers on the pulse and have a point-of-view on the industry?

    Because then our CIO customer will have more trust in what we say.

3. Why is it important to our CIO customer to have more trust in what we say?

    Because developments in our industry are changing quickly. Our customers need a trusted partner to keep them on top of what's going on.

4. Why does our CIO customer need a trusted partner to keep them on top of what's going on in our industry?

    Because they are busy trying to be successful, and a trusted partner can help them be informed.

5. Why is it important for our CIO customer's success to be informed?

   Because if they're informed about the industry from a trusted source, they will be more competitive—and can then be more successful.

Interesting. Within five "whys" we go from a blog that's focused on "positioning us as thought leaders" to a blog platform that "*helps our customers be more competitive and successful.*" That's value to THEM. Now, here's the intriguing part. You can go back and read those "whys" in reverse; with a little massaging and wordsmithing, you'll have a pretty well-formed vision (or content mission) for your story.

Now let's look at our example and run it backward. (Yes, we've massaged this a little.)

Our Mission:

CIOs are busy, and more than ever they need a trusted advisor that will help them be more competitive and successful in their career. They need to be kept up to date with a fast-changing industry, and the evolving trends in the business. Our new content curation news platform strengthens the trust our customer has in us. Our goal is to help our CIO customer think of OUR BRAND as the knowledgeable advisor that keeps his/her finger on the pulse of the industry.

See how it started with "why" (our core value) and worked backward to get to our original idea?

If you wanted to dig deeper, you could continue to ask more questions. For example, *"Why is it important that our customers are more competitive?"* Each "why" takes a bigger and more important leap toward understanding the larger context of the customer's world.

This is an important point. You'll notice that in the questioning, we immediately put the emphasis on *"why"* this is important to the audience. Creating value for them is the central point here. It's not about us creating value for us.

Now, not every idea is gold. In many instances you'll find that the "whys" lead to something that's not terribly interesting, so you can safely abandon the idea. But it's the process that's important. Just like with a child, developing the "whys" helps the inquisitive mind learn how to solve problems in a creative way. And, **most importantly, it encourages the entrepreneurial idea of the joy of discovery. This becomes central to breeding a culture of innovation.**

Additionally, we can start to take these "core values" and determine if they can be expressed uniquely, or differentiated, for our brand. They become testable product ideas that can be researched.

As Proust once said, *"The real voyage of discovery consists not in seeking new lands, but seeing with new eyes."* Asking *"why"* can certainly open them wider.

Okay, so we have the *"why"* and the *"who"* for this particular vision, and we can look to see if our new idea is differentiated and aligned with our overall brand promise. Now we need to develop the *"what."*

STEP 2: SET THE OBJECTIVE FOR THE VISION

As part of the framing of our new experience, we need to provide the reason why this "something" should be executed. So, the next step is to construct a definition of "what" we will create. To begin, we should start asking ourselves some important questions to assess the business value of the idea.

- **What business goal can we meet by creating this value?** What are we trying to accomplish with this? Don't confuse this with the success of the platform. The goal should be stated as a measurable business achievement (as outlined in Chapter 10). For example, drive X% more leads in X time. Or, create X% uplift in brand awareness. Or, create X% more value to the shopping cart.

- **What does success look like?** When we launch a new product, we don't expect it to hit sales goals two days after launch. Why do we expect the same of our content experiences? True success is almost never measured by when we launch an initiative, or even after we've had it "live" for some time. Success is achieved when we reach and sustain a minimally acceptable goal (or are highly confident that we will). Platform success may ultimately support more than one business goal—but only AFTER the platform has become successful.

So, "minimally" is an important concept there. Too often, we set business goals based on what we "hope" the platform can achieve, or without knowing that even a big success will be woefully inefficient to affect the business. So, we start the map by projecting the minimally acceptable goal for success of the platform itself and THEN draw a picture of what success looks like when we meet this goal.

- **How good are we at delivering this value?** In many cases, we are just building onto a brand promise that we are already making through other channels. So, in this case, it's just about executing in a more focused and compelling way. However, it could also be that we are trying to remediate some brand damage (e.g., think of a PR crisis management situation). Or, our brand doesn't have the "permission" to be extended to that value. For example, with all due respect, The Olive Garden restaurant is unlikely to be trusted as a tastemaker for fine Italian wines no matter what new content they put out. But could they use content to position themselves as a teacher of Italian wines more broadly? Well, maybe they can but it would fundamentally shift *the purpose of content they would launch with*. If we were the content marketers at The Olive Garden, we'd most likely need to change a lot of beliefs FIRST.

We need to honestly assess our ability to deliver the value of the core story in order to estimate how long it's going to take us to get there—or whether it can ever get us there. This will primarily affect the balance of our purpose-driven content mix.

- **How can we differentiate and deliver a different experience?** This is really where the channel discussion should happen. Just because there already *is* a blog on the topic we want to cover doesn't mean that we can't launch a new topical blog. But, how will our approach be different? What can, or should, we add? Can we also differentiate on HOW we deliver the story?

- **How can this story become cross-channel and cross-functional?** In other words, ask yourself how this idea will not only work across a blog or the sales function, but also across brand, public relations, social media, and other functions of the business. The best ideas are the ones that span the entire organization.

One of our favorite tips for this came from a conversation with Jonathan Mildenhall, former VP of worldwide creative and advertising for Coca-Cola. Mildenhall had a mandate that any team pitching to him must first consider how the idea would be cross-functional. As a result, many teams obtained buy-in from the cross-functional team leads early on, and already had input on where the ideas could—or should—be executed. This is a great example of "inspiring the revolution" that we discussed in Chapter 6.

Of course, you may think of additional questions that will help you draw a crisp and powerful argument for the business reasons behind an initiative. But, theoretically, you now have the insight to fill out the first two pieces of the story map.

Our next step is to look at "how" the map will be planned and executed.

STEP 3: SET THE MAP TO REALIZE THE VISION

Once the initiative has a vision and a business reason to exist, we must then make it real. As we've discussed, there are important differences in the way that marketing groups construct plans for campaigns vs. a content marketing approach.

In a traditional marketing or advertising campaign, we want to understand the campaign goals and tracking, the target audience, the key campaign messages, the offers, the media strategies, and the schedule and campaign integration. Many of these are similar to the construction of a content marketing approach.

But there is one critical—and often overlooked—difference. This experience really has no end. It's not a campaign. It's a content product.

In this regard, the mapping, building, and ultimate management of the content-driven experience looks much more like product development than it does a traditional marketing campaign.

We've examined in the previous step how to frame this initiative for addition to the business's portfolio. We've defined an idea, created a core proposed value for the audience, and created a business goal and a timeframe to reach both. These will now form the basis for creating the map for how to execute the initiative.

The mapping step is vital in executing an effectively managed content marketing initiative. It should be managed differently than a traditional marketing campaign, because we will need to create measurement strategies that enable us to launch it, modify it, manage it, and then sustain or decommission through the lens of permanence. The first operational difference is to change the order in which the planning will take place. Normally, when creating a marketing campaign or project, the first thing we do is discuss the milestones in the following order:

The Traditional Marketing Campaign Process

How long will this take to create/build?

(e.g., project plan, creative, technology, deployment)

Once we launch the effort, what will it take to manage it?

(e.g., what are the channels, content, technology, analytics, media)

What are our goals after the launch?

(Month one, two, three, etc., and then by the end of the campaign)

In fact, almost all digital projects done in concert with agencies are handled in exactly this way. The implemented methodologies are almost always some form of the following:

- Develop requirements for the project

- Design and implement based on those requirements

- Launch (or delay) based on the fulfillment of those requirements

- Manage and add in "phased aspects"

- Measure, learn, and reiterate, or begin again.

Thus, the way most marketing project-campaign plans are assembled and executed is based on a "best-case" scenario with go/no-go decisions based on how far along (or behind) the pre-prescribed timeline of the project is.

No doubt, many successful marketing campaigns and projects have been delivered this way. We are not suggesting that every marketing project methodology needs to be upended and changed into what Agile, the Lean Startup, or other methodologies would prescribe.

However, one of the key differences from traditional marketing campaigns is that content marketing initiatives are infused into the other communications efforts. In most cases, they need to be:

- Promoted and marketed

- Cross-functional

- Cross-channel

- Centered on fast adaptation.

Some of the biggest complaints about content marketing initiatives derive from common myths:

- They can't be measured or assessed until they've been live for a year (not true).

- We can't tie content-driven experiences to successful measurement for the business (not true).

- We're not structured to enable a company-wide content market-ing or customer experience mission (not true, even if silos exist).

In contrast to our description of traditional and familiar methodological initiatives, here is an alternative approach to mapping a content marketing initiative.

Starting with "X" Marks the Spot: Backward Mapping

Borrowing somewhat from the interesting work of Rita Gunther McGrath and Ian C. MacMillan, which is presented in their book, *Discovery-Driven Growth: A Breakthrough Process to Reduce Risk and Seize Opportunity*, we begin the story mapping step by starting at the end.

McGrath and MacMillan suggest starting a product development process by creating what they call a "reverse income statement," which allows you to:

> "…model how all the various assumptions in the initiative affect one another and whether, as you gain new information, the plan is getting traction or is at risk. The documents are intended to change as you learn, not to be a finished product."

Story mapping takes the reverse income statement idea and synthesizes it, using ideas from the concept of "backward design," and transforms it into an idea we call "backward mapping." What this means is that we start with our "X" that marks the spot, and then work backward.

Contextualizing "X"

Using the goal and the timeline we've established, we have an endpoint and know what a minimally viable success looks like at a relative point in time. What we don't know yet is how the timeline looks in context with what we must do to reach the endpoint.

To get there, we have to look at that point in time and make assumptions and draw conclusions about what needs to be true to achieve the vision that we set in Step 1.

For example, let's use the case of the B2B technology services company that we used earlier. In this example, the company rejected the "curated news" idea and decided to create an original content platform that targeted new, young, and ambitious CIOs (a core audience persona for them). Let's map out their story. Let's start with a recap of what we've learned so far and review their vision.

THE VISION

The "Why"

The Core Story (Our Content Mission)

> **a. Who is the audience for this story?**
> Young, ambitious CIOs who are looking to further their careers by keeping up with trends in IT.

> **b. What is the content mission (or core story)?**
> We can be the new voice of the CIO. Our MissionCriticalByDesign.com online magazine helps

CIOs navigate the fast-changing technology landscape. We help them stay current by reporting on the most important future trends in data center management and how they can navigate their career. Through original and curated content, we will be different than any other technology magazine out there in order to help the young CIO navigate a successful career.

c. **What is the narrative timeline for this story until success?**

We have no base for this because this is a new audience for us. So, we will first need to attract an audience for this platform and focus on audience development as a core strategy. We will first try to pull them in by leveraging industry influencers as guest writers. Then, to establish our authority, we will source great thought leadership content so essential to our audience that it will create a loyal base. Our narrative will have three parts: Inspire, Engage, and Accelerate. In alignment with our business case, we believe this will take 12 months from go-live to reach success.

The "What"

The Business Case

a. **What is the business goal?**

We achieve success when we are drawing 25% more monthly qualified leads from this new target persona. Additionally, 1,000 new engaged CIOs from our target company list will become aware of our brand and subscribe to our platform.

b. How will we differentiate our approach?

Our research has shown that no one is currently publishing a career-oriented magazine for young, ambitious CIOs who are trying to focus on mission-critical businesses. Our ability to connect these CIOs, as well as provide thought leadership on big data and data portability, gives us a unique advantage to deliver this value. We will also differentiate by making our online magazine available over mobile and social platforms.

c. How will we integrate this into our existing marketing or cross-functional efforts?

A key effort here, as part of our Inspire, Engage, Accelerate program, will be to introduce and promote this initiative through our existing direct marketing program, as well as through our onboarding program with new clients. We will work closely with our PR team to generate news that makes influencers and other industry luminaries aware of our new platform. Ultimately, this will integrate with the demand generation team to provide more qualified leads.

This map is very truncated, but it should give you an idea of where we would be when we start the actual mapping process. There's a very real business goal in this initiative. There's a narrative story present as well, because our example company realizes that their character (the brand) isn't known for this yet. They must first inspire, then engage this new audience, and finally create something scalable.

So, we begin the mapping process by defining what success looks like. Building on this definition, we make some assumptions and draw conclusions about what must be true. Thus, in the above example, we define success as:

- *Success:* when we have 25% more qualified leads and 1,000 new CIOs subscribed to our platform (e.g., brand awareness in our new target market).

With success clearly in sight, we work backward (in whatever granularity makes sense) to look at two things:

- What needs to be true at each stage (Inspire, Engage, and Accelerate)

- What assumptions we will need to make (a list of our best guesses using our experience and previous knowledge) about the best way to get to each truth.

Working from "X" backward, we split these into three discrete groups:

- Our business goals

- Our editorial mix of purpose-driven content

- Our integration mix into other areas of the business.

There may be others you might want to capture, and certainly this model can be expanded. The point is to capture, in categories, what the team needs to feel comfortable about moving forward.

If we designed a matrix defining the specific categories for our example, it would look like this (remember, we're working backward):

Accelerate Days 365 Forward		
Business Goals	**Editorial Mix**	**Integration Mix**
• 25% more qualified leads in the pipeline • 1,000 subscribers • 2,000 visitors to the platform	• 80% professor content • 10% poet content • 10% preacher and promoter content	• Core element of demand generation • Working with customer onboarding to expand into loyalty • Working with PR to attract new influencers to the platform
Engage II Days 270-365		
Business Goals	**Editorial Mix**	**Integration Mix**
• 1,000 visitors • 500 subscribers • 10% more qualified leads • User survey indicating strong CIO presence as subscribers	• 60% professor content to feed existing subscribers • 40% percent promoter or preacher content to continue promotion and audience acquisition	• Heavy integration with PR and Social for promotion • Promotion through email and client events • Standard part of client services onboarding program
Engage I Days 180-270		
Business Goals	**Editorial Mix**	**Integration Mix**
• 500 visitors • 200 subscribers • Some new qualified leads • Audience survey indicating valuable platform	• 40% professor content to feed clients • 60% promoter and preacher to promote program	• Heavy integration with PR and Social for promotional and influencer effort • Paid media opportunities to focus on audience acquisition • Email and web team key to making sure we are promoting new platform

Inspire 0-180 Days		
Business Goals	**Editorial Mix**	**Integration Mix**
• 500 total visitors • Three new influencer posts	• 80% promoter and preacher content • 10% professor content	• Full integration with PR and Social as blog launch, and integration with advertising team for paid media opportunities • Integration with event and other marketing services

As you can see, our content mix changes markedly as we move through the different phases. We start out with a ton of promotional content as we focus on audience development. This obviously affects our editorial strategy as well as our ability to generate leads. Then, as we reach success, we can dial down the promotional content while we accelerate the reasons why our audience should return and engage with our content.

Remember these are percentages, not quantities. So our content load at the beginning will be VERY high as we fill the blog AND the promotional channels. This helps us identify where the costs and budgets should be placed.

With this in mind, we can clearly communicate and inspire our teams and our C-suite, and propose a reasonable budget, timeline, and measurable strategy that will move our business forward.

If we've carefully planned our map, we should be well on our way to success. Because this is a process, we can anticipate that new tests and challenges will get in our way. So, we must also be prepared to make iterative changes along the way, based on both successes and failures.

STARTING THE JOURNEY

Deploying the initiative is really the meat of our narrative. If we set up the story well, success may simply flow from executing exactly as planned. Or, as is most often the case, it may mean improvising based on a sudden unplanned challenge or obstacle.

One of the keys here is to get into a review cycle—not based on major development milestones—but rather as a function of progress toward the different phases of the story as you have mapped it. The level of granularity of these rhythmic review cycles will depend largely on how confident you are about your assumptions, your learning along the way and, of course, the size of your investment in the initiative.

This process differs from campaign or classic marketing project planning because there are no "preconceived" stages that measure the project. Rather, we treat this as an approach, moving it forward based on our learning rather than on predetermined notions of success.

Checkpoints on this learning are the direct result of the goals we set in the vision or as other unpredictable changes arise.

At each checkpoint, we must ask very specific questions as a group and have ongoing discussions about continuing "as-is," with "modification to the plan," or by accelerating or decelerating the plan.

Questions to Ask

- What was the outcome we were hoping for?

- What was the reality we got?

- What did we learn from the gap, or the surplus?

- What do we need to change from our original assumptions?

- What do we need to change to meet the next business goal?

Using the measurement philosophy we describe in Chapter 10, you can start to look at your goals, your primary indicators, and your user indicators to get a good sense of how to report progress to others.

Don't Wait for Big Experiments; Prototype Early and Often

When creating the map, try to identify the "show stoppers" and those that can easily be tested. In other words, as we make assumptions, we will be making some of them with a high degree of confidence about their accuracy. Other assumptions, however, will be pure guesswork. Still others will be guesses that could be tested in advance.

For example, let's suppose one of the assumptions was that we could actually attract these new CIOs through a paid campaign to a number of existing CIO resources. This is something that could be tested and included as part of the story map. This might be especially important if instead of 1,000 subscribers, we were looking to address *10,000* subscribers. That paid campaign might be the biggest cost of our new initiative. Knowing how effective a paid campaign would be will be critical in understanding the timeline of the success of the initiative. We should plan on taking lots of little steps as we build toward a larger approach.

Remember, we are building toward the minimal acceptance of success. Even if we "blow it out of the water" initially, there may be unexpected challenges ahead. We still need to have review checks to see if our assumptions will be affected.

As we've mentioned, there are other, more detailed models for developing methodologies to deliver everything from small projects to enormous products. We've made no secret that our story mapping process borrows from a number of them. The key is to actually adopt one and scale it. Develop your own toolkit for the management of the content and your owned-media platforms. Once you have an actual process—a method by which to govern your actions—you will have the freedom to be more creative, more "outside the box," and more agile.

We don't know what's coming. All we know is that things will change. And if we structure ourselves to accommodate change, we will succeed in the long run.

WHAT'S NEXT: THE 90-DAY VISION

Story mapping can be a very valuable process—if not for project planning, for building a business case for a new initiative. But, the difference is that a story map is the plan (or business case) for a new "content product," not a campaign.

- The First Month

    Work with the CCM team to develop parts one and two of the story map.

    o **Define the content experience mission.** What is the valuable experience that is separate from your product or service? To whom will you deliver this value? Is it a differentiated experience? If not, how will you differentiate?

- o **Define the business goals.** Work toward one or multiple business goals that could be achieved by delivering this differentiated approach to this customer. What goals might it achieve in the first phase vs. how it might evolve over months or even years? What does success look like (separate from your business goals) and how long will it take to achieve? How will this success (or can it) be integrated into other parts of the customer's journey or your organization?

- The Second Month

Work with the CCM team to prioritize and outline the actual story map.

- o What does the narrative outline look like? Do you need to start with one type of content (such as poet content) to change beliefs before you start educating? Or, do you need to create awareness first, and then start bonding emotionally? What does the storyline look like over time? How does that comport with your business goals?

- o Are the business goals aligned with the level of effort needed to implement and integrate this initiative? What does this look like in the short term and over the long term?

o How will this story express itself through channels over time? How does this affect the purpose-driven content strategy?

- The Third Month and Onward

Create the implementation and integration plan and begin to manage the platform.

o Once budgets and the project are approved, work with the CCM team to assign resources for the "product development" of the initiative. How will the roll-out, plus the ongoing management, affect resources from marketing, subject matter experts, content sources, technology, etc.?

o Map the rollout and execute not based on major development milestones, but rather as a function of progress toward the different phases of the story as you have mapped it.

o Conduct frequent iterative reviews to establish whether "truths" have been reached and if changes are necessary in order to make future assumptions come true.

chapter 8:
WHY INTERNAL MARKETING IS THE FIRST AND LAST THING YOU SHOULD EVER DO

"Be the change you want to see in the world." | Mahatma Gandhi

At its core, marketing is about communicating. It's about getting people's attention, saying something interesting that matters to them, and then motivating them to change their behavior, attitude, or take action.

We focus a lot of our time and attention on outside audiences, which makes sense. We're trying to get people to buy what we sell. We want them to get to know us, like us, talk about us, and think that what we sell benefits them. Our marketing performance is based on how much, and in what ways, we're moving the needle with building, engaging, and retaining audiences.

That's an awful lot of heavy lifting, and to be truthful, marketing departments cannot do it all by themselves. There's so much going on within our organizations that it's hopeless to think that we can keep our finger on the pulse of everything. It's what David Packard, one of the founders of Hewlett-Packard, understood when he said, *"Marketing is too important to be left to the marketing department."*

We spend so much time telling our story externally that it's easy for us to forget about the most important audience we have—our fellow employees. However, if our primary goal is to own niches, online and off, we have to teach employees how to help tell our story.

We know that customers have relationships with people, not brands. So marketers need to take a leadership role in helping employees understand what makes a company special, especially the employees who interact directly with customers. As we look to create seamless, meaningful experiences for customers, employees turn into more than brand ambassadors; they become promise-keepers. They're the ones who bring to life the promises made by marketing and sales.

One of our roles as content marketers needs to be getting our employees, the people who bring our brands to life, excited about the story we are telling. More than believing in it, we want them to join in creating the experiences that make the story real, so that marketers and employees all sing in harmony.

Hail, Hail, What if the Gang's *Not* All Here?

To win customers (and a bigger share of the marketplace), companies must first win the hearts and minds of their employees. To be successful at this, marketers must understand the need to build a group that's accountable for consistent publishing for *internal* audiences and that works shoulder to shoulder with what we do on the outside.

Kathy Button Bell, vice president and chief marketing officer of Emerson, talks about marketing's ability to create emotion within a company. She describes it as a function of bringing color, light, and movement. For her, how we adapt to telling brand stories to different audiences, through multiple channels, is connected to the story's ability to create joy and something to which we should aspire. It used to be enough for us to make sure that employees knew what the logo looked like, but now we need to move into creating valuable experiences for our own people. Today, the need for someone to take responsibility for a consistent employee experience is more important than ever. And, marketing brings the power of that consistency.

As we examine our internal roles, more and more we are becoming stewards of story and culture. The internal culture of a company determines so much when it comes to the destiny and position of marketing.

But does focusing this much on the inside audience really make that much of a difference? Absolutely.

Gallup's 2013 *State of the Global Workplace* looked at high-performance, world-class organizations.[70] In surveying more than 225,000 employees in 142 countries around the world, they found that only 13% of employees worldwide were engaged in their work. That's an improvement of only 2% from their survey in 2008–2009. That leaves a staggering 87% either not engaged, or actively disengaged, which is a big deal when you start to translate that into financial performance. However, the survey found that high-performance companies earned nearly four times more than their industry competitors and experienced one-third less attrition.

People spend a majority of their waking hours at their jobs, and it doesn't matter if it's a local landscaping company, a high-tech startup, or a financial institution. That's why the depth of employee engagement reflects how people feel about their jobs and the quality of the work they produce.

Gallup found that the majority of employees worldwide said they had an overall negative experience at work; just one in *eight* were fully involved in, and enthusiastic about, their jobs. And actively *disengaged* employees outnumbered *engaged* employees two-to-one.

Performance problems don't just affect disengaged employees. Gallup also pointed out that 41% of U.S. employees don't know what their employer stands for or what makes their company different from others. While people are less scared about actually keeping their jobs these days, they aren't confident about what work, exactly, they're *supposed* to be doing.[71]

As marketers, we need to increase our role and influence on increasing employee purpose and engagement, because increasing it is crucial to driving sustainable growth for our companies.

So, what exactly do we have the ability—and right—to influence?

EMPLOYEES, CUSTOMERS, AND REVENUE

Research shows that there is a direct link between employee satisfaction and customer satisfaction, and between customer satisfaction and improved financial performance by a company. Organizations with satisfied and engaged employees motivate customers to use their products more. And, increased customer usage leads to higher levels of customer satisfaction.

Research also shows that an organization's employees influence the behavior and attitudes of customers, even if the employees don't have direct contact with customers. Employees who don't have direct contact often think they don't influence customers, but they do. Their hard work behind the scenes makes for positive customer influence. Ultimately, the most satisfied customers turn out to be less expensive to serve, to use the products more, and to be more profitable.

Professional services firm Towers Watson, in its 2012 *Global Workforce Study*, talked about the difficulty of sustaining the kind of positive engagement that employees need in order to deliver consistent productivity.[72] This comes from almost a *decade* of pressure to do more with less and to respond to the challenges of global competition, ever-evolving technology, and the ongoing need to strictly control costs.

When workers aren't fully engaged, it leads to greater performance risk for employers. It makes companies more vulnerable to lower productivity, higher inefficiency, weaker customer service, and greater rates of absenteeism and turnover. When Towers Watson looked at sustainable engagement for 50 global companies, and their one-year operating margins, they saw dramatic evidence of the impact of sustainable engagement on performance. The companies with high, sustainable engagement had operating margins almost *three times* greater than those of organizations with a largely disengaged workforce.

In Gallup's research, those companies with the highest levels of engagement experienced 147% higher earnings per share, compared with their competition. And those with a low level of employee engagement experienced 2% lower earnings per share, compared with their competition. Active disengagement has an immense drain on economies throughout the world. In the U.S. alone, Gallup estimated that active disengagement costs companies $450-500 *billion per year*.

Employees have to be engaged in order to understand and articulate their company's uniqueness. Why should a customer do business with a company when employees can't explain what makes them different and better? It doesn't matter how much is invested in external marketing; if the customer experience with employees is negative, then it's all gone to waste.

Here's how it pans out if employees *really* had a choice about keeping their jobs. Gallup asked U.S. workers, "If you won $10 million in the lottery, would you continue to work, or would you stop working? If 'continue to work,' would you continue to work in your current job, or would you take a different job?"

Here's how the responses came out:

	Actively disengaged	Not engaged	Engaged
Continue in current job	20%	42%	63%
Take a different job	41%	25%	12%
Stop working	40%	33%	25%

Despite all the statistics describing what happens when employees aren't engaged and telling the same story about our business, why don't we put the same level of care and effort into communicating with our entire company as we do with customers and prospects? If our team isn't telling the same story and creating a seamless customer experience, all we've invested in branding, public relations, marketing, sales, and customer service is a joke. If we need a business case for investing in our story internally, think of it as insurance to protect all the other investments we've made.

WHERE TO BEGIN

Where do we start with getting everyone to sing the same song, much less in harmony? We're going to walk through three big-picture steps to help give context for the breadth and depth of what needs to be done.

Start with the leaders

These are the senior people who can help drive the story from the top down, and they know how to get people involved with a program. Regular communication from the company's leaders will begin to breed a culture of engagement. If it's a big company, communication has to come from both the enterprise and local levels. Executives set the direction of the company based on the story, but transformation and bringing that story alive happens at the local level.

How do we get executives to pay attention to the importance of this? We have to speak their language: financial performance.

In their book, *Built to Last*, Jim Collins and Jerry Porras pointed out that companies driven by purpose—and that have the values in place to support that purpose—outperform the general market 15 to one. And, they outperform comparison companies six to one.[73] John Kotter and James Heskett, in *Corporate Culture and Performance*, also noted that companies that have cultures based on purpose and values outperform companies that don't: their research showed that revenues grew four times faster, job creation was seven times greater, and stock prices grew 12 times faster.[74]

Second, look for your connectors

These are the people who *really* know the ins and outs of an organization—the ones who can make or break a project, not because they are in positions of power, but because they have influence. It's what Malcolm Gladwell talks about in his book, *The Tipping Point*. Among the different types of personalities he describes are the "connectors." They are the people who know everyone. They bring people together. And if they believe in the brand story, they can help others do the same.[75]

Third, focus on the people who will be most affected by the story

These are the people who really have to "live" the story because they're the ones bringing it to life for customers. Think customer experience service professionals, the people in accounting—people who customers talk to but who we don't traditionally think of as being the ones who make experiences come alive for customers.

Make your story understandable and captivating for people.

Bring the brand story into everyday language using everyday words. Communicate the "why" of the story to employees. Use words, phrases, and anecdotes they can relate to. For example, why does the strategic direction being taken matter to them? How does their role fit into the bigger picture? What contribution can they make on an individual basis? Skip the corporate speak and explain it in the same way you would if you were talking to a real person.

Find ways to tell the story in the places where people are. Think about the influences of local cultures and economics as well as factors such as an employee's type of job and education level. They all play a role in how employees share the story.

As the story is rolled out, get people excited about it and keep them excited *after* they first hear about it. They can be the eyes and ears on the ground for what's working and where the effort is running into challenges with people who don't believe it or support the story. Look for excuses to tell your story again and again and tie it into things your company does. Are you launching a new product? Explain how that came about in the context of the bigger brand story. Win a hard-to-snag client? Why was their belief in your brand purpose the reason that your sales team sealed the deal?

Internal communications have to be just as much fun—*and human* (if not more so)—as external stories. Get rid of the urge to "business speak" this to death. Skip talking about how this will optimize performance, maximize productivity, or other "ize" buzzwords that make this sound like corporate ramblings. Instead, create online and real-time conversations with people on a human and emotional level.

When reviewing brand efforts for 2014, Antonio Lucio, global chief marketing and communications officer for Visa, and his team scrutinized the communications they had created for employees with the same rigor they did for B2C and B2B audiences. "*We looked to see if we're delivering a comprehensive and integrated brand message,*" he said. "*We want to know that we're making our employees true spokespeople for our brand.*" [76]

Let's look at four specific areas that have a big impact on how engrained the brand story is within an organization: human resources, sales, research and development (or the people who decide what to sell and how to evolve it over time), and the overall employee population.

1. Human Resources

One of the expanding opportunities for telling brand stories can be found in human resources. Many companies fall short on doing a good job of communicating with current employees, much less extending the brand story to those they hope to recruit. But, hiring the right people is essential to building a workforce that's truly engaged in what your company does.

If we thought of supporting human resources as a way to recruit people to deliver our brand story, marketers would be more proactive in working with them. That's because these recruits are the filters through which we'll build our own teams. Research from The FORUM, the research arm of the Business Marketing Association, shows that within the next five years, Millennials will outnumber Baby Boomers in the workplace by two to one. That's a huge cultural shift in a short amount of time. It means that we need to be ready to help human resources communicate with four generations of workers: Baby Boomers, Gen X, Gen Y, and Millennials.

In order to have the right people tell the right story, we have to hire the right people. That means telling our story consistently through all channels, not just to reach customers but to reach prospective employees, too. We need to consider the human resources angle when we work on top-of-funnel awareness. The stories that matter to customers also matter to the rock stars we want to recruit. These involve ideas such as culture, leadership, challenge, and growth.

In competitive industries and job markets, recruiting top-tier talent is crucial. But despite its importance, it can be easily overlooked because of pinched resources and day-to-day job demands.

A report from the Altimeter Group surveyed human resources and marketing executives from both B2B and B2C companies. Among the results:

- Only 41% of respondents said their company has a holistic and strategic approach to employee engagement and advocacy.

- HR leads the employee engagement efforts in 41% of the companies and only 11% are led by marketing.

- On the flip side, marketing is involved in 47% of the actual employee engagement initiatives and human resources only 39%.[77]

Fortunately, we can partner with human resources not only to tell our brand story through them, but also to discover stories about why people come to work for us, what matters to them, and how their own stories mesh with the brand story. This gives us insight into how our content marketing makes a difference in recruiting the right people and the importance of our work within our organizations. However, marketers need to take a greater leadership role because of all of the best practices we bring to the table: how to drive and measure engagement, how to create delightful experiences, how to nurture audiences, and how to tell a story that keeps people interested and engaged over a long period of time. HR professionals, on the other hand, realize that they lack these skills: only 42% of chief human resource officers believe they're effective at fostering employee engagement and a mere 20% think they have what it takes to effectively address collaboration and information-sharing challenges.[78]

The connection with audiences and building an employee retention relationship is nicely conceptualized by the content marketing hourglass created by Robert Rose and Joe Pulizzi, and described in their book *Managing Content Marketing.* We need a well-thought-out process that identifies the right people to recruit, in the same way that we create personas for our customers, and their potential role within the organization. We work with them in the same way that we segment external audiences. We can then understand how to nurture them and convert them to employees.

But it doesn't stop there.

Many employers treat the conversion from recruit to employee the same way as the honeymoon period in a new marriage: Once they sign on the dotted line, the romance fades and they're left with the drudgery of everyday life. But, long, happy marriages prevail when both sides understand the importance of communication and jointly build a common story. So, just because a person begins to work for us doesn't mean we can ignore their interests and concerns. We must keep communication open and build the story, the relationship, and the experiences. We need to get creative about engaging with employees so that we can nurture them and evolve them from people who are merely satisfied with their work to loyal employees, and eventually to brand evangelists.

Keep telling your brand story once people start working for your company. Will a company intranet and an annual town hall meeting cut it? Probably not. Because we live in an instant, real-time world, you should consider incorporating enterprise social network tools such as Yammer and Socialcast. Even Google+ supports internal hangouts and lets people post only within their organization. Companies that have nontraditional, hard-to-reach employees such as medical staff, oil rig workers, or field-tech teams, have started to develop "bring your own device" policies, so employees can connect online using their mobile device of choice. After all, employees can learn to tell the brand story only if the company can connect with them.

VISITORS

APPLICANTS

RECRUITS

OPPORTUNITIES

ACCEPTANCE

EMPLOYEES

SATISFY

RETAIN

LOYAL

PROMISE KEEPERS

VISITORS

Nurturing prospective employees into engaged brand evangelists is a process similar to nurturing prospects into loyal customers.

2. Sales

Salespeople are the face of any company. Many come to marketing and ask for help because they're starting to understand social selling and the idea of social business. They want to be able to write blog posts, comment in online forums, connect with people on LinkedIn, and post presentations to SlideShare.

Sadly, for many salespeople it's easier to do a Google search to find out what their own company is saying, rather than try to hear it from marketing. This is because there's no organized structure for how marketing publishes content internally, how it's organized, or how the sales team can find and use it. There's just a glut of "stuff" that salespeople don't have time to dig through. There's no company emphasis on helping them understand why it's important to be consistent or how doing so can improve their performance.

We know that buyers today are up to 70% of the way through their decision-making process before they reach out to a salesperson.[79] But up to 60% of all buying decisions are lost to the status quo—meaning the prospect decides to stay with what he already has instead of making a change.[80] That's a huge red flag.

It means that marketing and sales must communicate more effectively, because while customers are *self-educated*, that doesn't mean that they're *well-educated*. Sales must be ready to tell the same story in a familiar language for customers before they come to the table and before the first direct sales conversation.

Corporate Visions points out that executive decision makers view salespeople as 88% proficient in their knowledge of products, but only

24% proficient on conversing about business challenges.[81] If you've successfully transitioned your marketing story into one that talks about solving problems and delivering business value, have you helped your sales team do the same?

We need a framework for better communication and feedback so that the stories we marketers tell actually prepare prospects for their first conversation with sales. Salespeople also need to speak up about what they need marketing to be communicating. According to the CMO Council, salespeople spend 40% of their time looking for or preparing content for customer communications. That's a lot of wasted time, which can lead to problems such as inconsistent messaging and inaccurate information. That time can be minimized with better marketing, sales, and customer communication.

We marketers generate a lot of resources around industry trends, business challenges, use cases, and best practices. A primary goal is to help position our brands as trusted sources of information. But it's equally important to make sure the sales teams are intimately familiar with our top-of-funnel strategy so that their conversations will be a much deeper extension of the same story. Several of our clients have implemented a marketing automation approach with their sales teams, so they can track behavior and understand engagement and nurturing for their sales teams through content. Just like data and analytics help inform marketers about what matters to customers, it can do the same internally with sales teams. We need to make sure that someone is covering the middle ground and that we aren't leaving prospects in "no man's land" between marketing and sales.

Towers Watson says that one of the benefits of building sustainable engagement within an organization is that high-performing sales

233

employees are almost twice as likely to be highly engaged than lower-performing sales employees. Teaching our sales team how to use the brand story for conversations beyond those at the top of the funnel will improve their ability to find opportunities to drive more business—and to improve their individual performance.

When we consider content such as customer examples, testimonials, product or service demos, and white papers, we must think about how to use these to help sales continue to tell the brand story later in the sales cycle. We also need to teach sales reps how to use content to sell more effectively. Moreover, this will help reduce the 40% time-suck, so they can spend more time doing what they do best—selling.

3. Research and Development

Marketers rarely see their role as a connecter and unifier, a role that begins with research and development. It's not just that R&D needs to know what's going on with the company in general, it's that marketing needs to take the brand story and start from the very beginning, not four steps down the road during focus groups, and help discover new ways to delight customers.

For example, Emerson's brand story revolves around solving problems for their customers. They took the voice of their customers and backed it up to everything they created and delivered. They realized that many of the answers to their customers' problems weren't new products, but rather more innovative approaches to how they did business. They saw that, as their customers became savvier, they looked for things such as efficiency, productivity, and cost savings because their own financial demands were stringent. They moved from producing only products to evangelizing the experience they were creating for customers and creating as simple and seamless an experience as they could.

This approach led to studying what mattered most to customers in a different light. For example, for one customer, solving their problems and simplifying business didn't come in the form of a new product. It was literally about how to do business together. In one instance, improvement came in the form of consolidated invoices that were easier to read. *Simple?* Perhaps. *Easy* to do for a global enterprise with numerous backend systems? Not exactly. But with the focus on solving problems for customers and simplifying business, teams within Emerson understood the need to collaborate across the company to make it possible.

4. Employees

When it comes to the overall employee population, we're consistently amazed at how many companies ignore this audience. Why does a company spend hundreds of thousands—sometimes *millions*—to brand or rebrand themselves and tell a story that they believe will make them stand out in a noisy marketplace, and then neglect teaching their all-important internal audience how to tell that story?

A recent study from Altimeter Group found that only 51% of employees clearly understood and supported the purpose and mission of their organization. Only 43% said their employer's culture was one of trust and empowerment that is needed for employee engagement and advocacy. Fewer than half (45%) said they knew what they should and shouldn't do around company-related topics on social media.[82]

Remarkable brand stories don't just get customers and prospects talking; it's also exciting for employees to hear and talk about their story.

Wonderful brand stories give people something to share with one another, something to banter back and forth, and something to champion. Those stories encourage people to open lines of communication and to hear different opinions and points of view.

When employees engage with the brand story, it's much easier to invite them to be a part of the story and contribute to it. When they take part in creating and telling that ongoing story, employees take greater ownership in making it come alive through experiences. They become deeply, emotionally engaged with the companies they work for, and create seamless experiences for external audiences.

Long, happy marriages between employers and employees happen when both sides understand the importance of communication and how to create their story together. So what, exactly, does that take in today's unpredictable environment?

Motorola Solutions serves as an example of how to do it right. The company functioned as one entity for 80 years under the Motorola name. In January 2011, Motorola split into two: B2B brand Motorola Solutions and consumer-facing Motorola Mobility, which Google later bought. Leadership had prepared for the separation for two years.

Motorola Solutions discussed the need to have a clear, compelling story that not only created engagement in their employees, but would also attract people to work for their company, retain employees, and keep them engaged for the long term. They wanted to know how to keep employees motivated and how to keep them focused. Most importantly, they wanted to tell the story of where they were going (as a company) to employees, so they could, in turn, bring it to life for customers.

They saw this as a time to teach employees how they could make a difference not only within the company, but also with their customers all around the world. They believed wholeheartedly that it would foster a sense of pride in the work that people did, while improving and enhancing their employee engagement.

From the employees' perspective, it started one Friday afternoon when they went home as employees of one company, and then on Monday, returned to work for one of two companies. Over the weekend, Motorola Solutions physically rebranded 30 of its facilities worldwide so that when employees walked in on Monday morning they saw tangible expressions of change—evidence that their new brand story was already coming to life.[83]

The company spent the rest of 2011 integrating the brand promise into the corporate culture and helping employees understand how to tell it to the outside world. They took their brand story, *"helping people be better in the moments that matter,"* and taught employees about the impact they had on the world and kept them excited about what the company did on a long-term, sustainable basis.

This was crucial, because as Motorola Solutions' focus shifted to telling the story externally, their ads, their website, and the content for sales and human resources told the story that employees already knew. So if a customer mentioned something about an ad, employees could easily continue the conversation and extend that story. Most importantly, customers could tell that Motorola Solutions employees *believed* in the story they were telling.

This employee "buy in" is important to understand. It's not unusual for a company's story to lack credibility with employees. If the brand story reflects the company today, employees will more easily engage as storytellers—*if it's a good story.* If we're trying to change the story being told, employees need tangible expressions of change, recruitment, recognition, rewards, and overall culture before they begin to believe. Marketing needs to help them feel proud to represent their employers. Fundamentally, it's vital that employees tell the company's story as a cohesive unified team.

CREATING A FRAMEWORK

Just as we strategically plan and manage the stories that we tell to audiences outside the company, we need to plan and structure how we manage content creation for internal audiences in the same way. It's a key part of how we create consistent conversations and experiences with employees.

In this illustration, we have the team (or person) who's responsible for internal content at the center. From there, we have four goals that they need to focus on to develop a successful content creation management system for employees.

- **At the top of the circle**, we need content marketers to focus on creating excitement for employees and inspiring them to be a part of learning our story and then, eventually, making it come alive.

- **Once we have their attention**, we move to the right to make sure that we consistently deliver the brand story over and over again. It has to be consistent through every channel where it's told: executive communication, company intranet, employee newsletters, all employee calls, the language that human resources uses around benefits, culture, rewards, and recognition—all channels. Our goal is to make sure that employees have a deep understanding of the brand story and what it means to them in their world. This might be human resources or sales, but it can also mean research and development, accounting, and IT; it has to resonate and feel real for employees in every department. We want to make it easy for every person to share and consume the story. Because the more the story is shared, the more it's reinforced and becomes engrained in the organization.

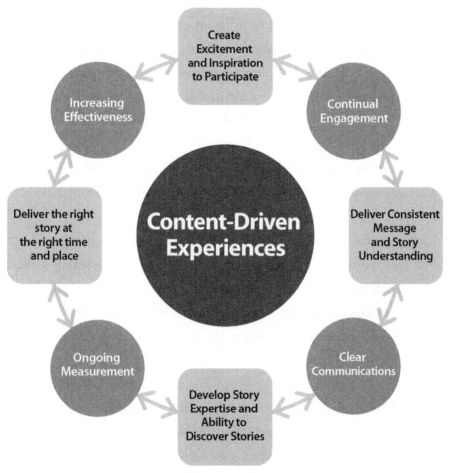

Marketers need a framework for internal publishing in order to create consistent conversations with employees.

- **Next, moving to the bottom of the circle**, we want employees to know the story *so* well that they have a deep expertise in it. That means that they're highly engaged in telling it and they'll help uncover new stories, both internally and with customers, that will resonate as the story is told.

- **And finally, just as with external audiences**, we have to make sure that we're delivering the right story to the right person, at the right time and place. Not *every* employee has to hear *every* story, nor do they want to. So we need to be discerning about how stories are told to different employee populations, so that we aren't creating noise for them, which will only make them tune out. They have limited attention spans, just like customers and prospects, and we need to make sure that we're talking about what's relevant in their world.

Now that we know the four areas to focus on, the internal content manager needs to understand some of the dynamics of this framework.

If the content manager focuses on creating continual engagement, that will transition employees from being excited and wanting to be a part of telling the brand story, to the next phase. This is where they're actively engaged and have a clear understanding of the brand story and understand how their work creates the actual experience that customers have.

From there, clearly communicate the story so that employees develop expertise in understanding and telling the story and can discuss the "why" behind it. They recognize when they see other examples of living and delivering that brand story, either in their own work or in that of others.

At this point, we can begin to measure the effectiveness of internal content efforts, how well employees retain the brand story, and how we can improve effectiveness. We can do this with internal audits, surveys, or focus groups to get a better sense of what we can do to increase overall effectiveness. We can then start to look for other opportunities to further engrain the brand story, so it becomes second nature. Following this model, content managers will be able to uncover stories that are hidden deeper within an organization—*better* stories—and begin to tell them internally and externally.

Finally, think about how to increase the effectiveness of what's being done to improve engagement and to make sure that people hear the stories that are the most relevant to them. This way, we can keep the excitement going for what the organization is doing and can solidify and grow relationships with employees, as they feel more and more part of the bigger whole that is the brand story.

WHAT'S NEXT: THE 90-DAY VISION

Marketers must understand that a key expansion of our role is to teach employees our brand story and help them make it come alive for external audiences. Empowering employees to become brand storytellers is critical to creating seamless experiences for all audiences outside the company.

- The First Month—Assessing the state of the union

    o Are you doing anything now to connect with employees? This may mean your intranet (in whatever way, shape, or form it's maintained—or not), departmental, or functional communications (e.g., human resources, updates to technical teams, communications with the field or front-line employees, channel partners, etc.). Make a complete audit of what's already being done, by whom, the audience, and frequency. Groups may continue to manage their micro-communities, but you still need to understand them and tap them to share what's going on with the greater employee population as needed.

o   Bring employees into your CCM strategy.

o   As you move through the CCM framework, identify the CCM team members responsible for internal publishing.

o   As you plan to organize and manage your CCM framework, keep in mind that employees are part of your audience. What experiences do you want to create for them?

o   Do you have any kind of baseline measurement? This may be employee engagement scores or feedback from employees about current communications programs now in place (think across the organization, not just those that may come from marketing or corporate communications).

• The Second Month—Infusing the story

o   Huddle with leadership and begin to get buy-in to breed a culture of engagement. If you work for a big company and need to cascade through the local level, understand who those key people are.

o Identify the connectors within your organization who can work magic because of their credibility and influence. Talk to them about your plan, your goals, their role, and pay attention to their insights and feedback.

o Understand who's most affected by your brand story. Where are you seeing the biggest gaps between how well you tell your brand story outside the company and how well it's actually executed internally? These are the people you need to start with, so they understand the bigger WHY of their work. Is sales telling a seamless story with marketing? Does the picture that human resources paint match the culture of your company? If you can check these boxes, begin digging deeper into customer service and operational performance.

o Include story mapping for employees as you go through this exercise during the second month of the 90-day vision for story mapping.

• The Third Month and Onward—Continual engagement

o Lay-out and story map a number of experiences. Collaborate on "if and how" they will benefit each function within the organization, and assemble the plan.

o Refer to your CCM framework to ensure that you're consistently driving relevant and delightful experiences clearly and effectively.

o Ensure that the brand voice uses everyday language, so it's interesting, fun, captivating, and enticing for employees.

o Measure the effectiveness of internal content efforts and how well employees are retaining the brand story; make adjustments to improve the performance of your content.

ENDNOTES

70   http://www.gallup.com/poll/165269/worldwide-employees-engaged-work.aspx

71   Liberman, Vadim. *Performance Anxiety,* The Conference Board Review, Spring 2014.

72   http://www.towerswatson.com/Insights/IC-Types/Survey-Research-Results/2012/07/2012-Towers-Watson-Global-Workforce-Study

73   Collins, Jim and Porras, Jerry. *Built to Last: Successful Habits of Visionary Companies,* Harper Business Essentials, 2004, Appendix. Numbers are based on the performance histories of brands that the authors identified as visionary companies and their comparison companies.

74   http://forbes.com/sites/johnkotter/2011/02/10/does-corporate-culture-drive-financial-performance

75   Gladwell, Malcolm. *The Tipping Point: How Little Things Can Make a Big Difference.* Bay Back Books, 2002.

76   Interview with Carla Johnson, December 19, 2014.

77   http://adage.com/article/btob/companies-employee-engagement-strategy/296257/?utm_content=buffer2a230&utm_medium=social&utm_source=twitter.com&utm_campaign=buffer

78   http://www.altimetergroup.com/2014/04/contribute-to-altimeters-report-on-employee-engagement-and-advocacy/

79   SiriusDecisions.

80   http://corporatevisions.com/resources/article-archive/why-your-sales-message-doesnt-work/

81   http://corporatevisions.com/the-right-skills/justification-skills/

82   http://adage.com/article/btob/companies-employee-engagement-strategy/296257/?utm_content=buffer2a230&utm_medium=social&utm_source=twitter.com&utm_campaign=buffer

83   https://www.youtube.com/watch?v=0A2LKjNC-gM Accessed November 17, 2014.

chapter 9:
CONTENT CREATION MANAGEMENT TECHNOLOGY: BUILT TO CHANGE

"It has become appallingly obvious that our technology has exceeded our humanity." | Albert Einstein

Ask any marketer what the two biggest trends disrupting business are and you'll likely get the answer "big data" and "customer centricity." For the technology-minded (e.g., our CIOs), this means an enormous amount of pressure to get business software to work seamlessly. CIOs must help the business take advantage of all the customer data they are accustomed to storing, while simultaneously developing new ways to manage new unstructured and transactional data. It's a process that can, in many cases, be overwhelming.

Likewise, marketing's mandate has expanded to now cover the creation of optimal experiences across every appropriate channel.

So, when it comes to technology to help facilitate all this disruption, you'd think the CMO and CIO would be best friends at this point—kindred spirits working together to bring these concepts together. You'd like to think they'd be like two kids riding in the back seat to Disneyland, working together to make the car go faster.

Yes, you'd like to think that.

But the reality is (as every parent knows) quite different. These days, the CMO and CIO are both screaming, "are we there yet?" from the back seat. The CMO is holding his finger in the CIO's face, saying, "not touching, not touching." And the CIO is saying, "mine, mine, mine" to every single thing the CMO picks up.

So, what can we do to ensure that we have a safe and productive ride? We've identified four layers, that when implemented well, can provide a bit of sanity to the CCM process.

FOUR LAYERS IN A CUSTOMER EXPERIENCE FOCUS

Both the marketing strategy and the tools that support it should make the customer's journey as easy and compelling as possible. It's the CIO's job to make that journey easy to facilitate, scalable, and flexible for the CMO's team. And it's the CMO's job to understand the design of the experiences so well that he or she can communicate the team's needs to the CIO. Together they have to focus on:

Awareness and introduction

Owned-media platforms like blogs, social, and websites are yesterday's media buy. Before the customer is even a "known" visitor, the marketer can create value by tracking the consumption of content and usage patterns to understand their interests and what is valuable to them.

The technology strategy here should be lightweight, flexible, and often disposable. Things change rapidly here. Collaboration with any number of external sources from people, channels, languages, and styles will be required. This is where marketers will need to move the fastest to be the most effective. In short: the CIO should care the least about this layer.

Engagement and relationship

As visitors become leads, more emphasis is needed on using data and the insight it can provide to develop a more delightful experience that will pay dividends down the road. The goal here is to inform every other part of the organization how the business can operate to meet and exceed customer expectations. This is where a unified customer experience management solution is so critical.

It's essential to have a management process here that can integrate into the fast-moving technology of the awareness and introduction stage, but also scale to meet the optimization, data, and insight requirements of every stage through to the CRM system. Put simply, the CMO needs to understand this process much more deeply and design more carefully here. This differs from the awareness stage. Thus, more care should be put into fewer experiences that change less often. A more holistic process is needed.

Intelligence and insight

After leads become customers, it is critical to develop a methodology and process that is centered on learning how customer's needs evolve. The focus should be not only on developing strategies to feed data back into the acquisition of new customers, but also on how to use that data to retain customers and upsell or cross-sell additional products and services. The ultimate goal is to create brand evangelists.

Here the technology and process must focus on how the customer experience system can draw data out of other, more enterprise back-end systems in order to optimize experiences for well-known customers. Integration is the key. The CIO must work with the CMO to understand "what data is needed" to optimize the experience, before developing the integration strategies to acquire the data.

Shared values and exceeded expectations

This is less of a physical layer and more of a final attribute that is the foundation of the other three. It involves developing a shared vision with both marketing and technology to see how partnering with customers and the business can become an integral part of the business strategy.

It is not enough for the CMO and CIO to understand one another's strategy and acronyms. The two teams must actively collaborate to develop a joint strategy for customer-centricity and the technology needed to facilitate it.

Ultimately, the goal of these four layers is to help the CMO and CIO understand and communicate the "approach" to technology and customer-centricity. It's easy for the CIO to get caught up in the "*we have a tool for that*" mindset and decide myopically that because it's a "content tool" it can solve any and every content problem. Conversely, the CMO can easily get wrapped up in the "*I need everything yesterday because it's always about more*" state of mind. Getting the marketing team to view "content as a process" (rather than "content as a campaign") will help everyone develop a more considered approach to deeper customer engagement infrastructures.

To summarize:

- The CMO should focus on the WHAT—and make it as compelling, relevant, and resonant as possible.

- The CIO should focus on the HOW—making it as fast, easy, and flexible as possible.

SOFTWARE SOLUTIONS: SOLVING THE WHAT AND HOW

Remember, only within the last six years has the enterprise needed to manage the explosion of digital content channels. Even up until the mid-2000s, the term web content management (WCM) described a system that would enable the organization to create, edit, publish, and deliver content to a singular (or, in some cases, multiple) website. This was simply making the organization more efficient at doing something it was already doing—managing content. However, as marketing and content have become more important, enterprise-class solutions for WCM, marketing campaign management, web analytics, and CRM have all been evolving to offer new "engagement" features.

Simultaneously, disruptive marketing tools that facilitated higher levels of content relevance, social conversation, and engagement began to emerge in the mid-2000s. Over the last six years, these tools have been maturing and finding their way into the marketer's toolbox. Software solutions for marketing automation, content testing and optimization, social publishing, and sentiment analysis have sprung up as disruptive replacements for old processes. These systems offer marketers new capabilities, while providing technology teams with even more systems to integrate into a cohesive new strategy.

While software vendors race to keep up with all of the different customer channels, methods, and interfaces that they must enable marketers to manage and monitor, marketing departments struggle to avoid technology overload. As one frustrated CMO exclaimed at the Forrester CIO-CMO Summit in 2013, *"I feel more like a CIO than a CMO! I have marketing automation, CRM, listening platforms. I'm up to my eyeballs in technology."* [84]

This confusion has led to years of chaos in the deployment of digital content, marketing, content optimization, social, and measurement systems across the enterprise. To address this, enterprises have usually adopted one of two strategies:

- **Rely on a rock-solid enterprise content management/digital marketing backbone technology.** Usually this project is a consolidation of smaller web content management systems, multiple marketing solutions, and perhaps early forays into social publishing and analytics. This global enterprise system provides the core functions to the marketing teams, which allows them to manage content, create campaigns, monitor success, and build out functionality—but prevents them from innovating quickly.

- **Deploy ad hoc "point solution" systems.** These technologies separately handle websites, blogging, content optimization, marketing automation, and social media management. More typical in midsized organizations, this is usually the result of "as needed" technology acquisition. The result is often small, cobbled-together integration. This is where the "CMO as CIO" feeling is most pronounced. These organizations have typically over-purchased technology. Many systems go underused or even forgotten, and are typically replaced as each new marketing requirement dictates.

The challenges for the marketing team with the enterprise backbone technology are that they are typically:

- Frustrated with the speed at which they can move

- Dissatisfied with the upgrades that the vendor is making (usually well behind the curve) and the agility they have shown

- Extremely dependent on their internal (or agency side) technology group for any new capabilities, publishing channels, or new processes they must facilitate.

The challenges with the ad hoc point solution system, however, are just as pronounced. In this case, the marketing team is:

- Frustrated by the lack of consistency between any two systems they've adopted

- Always behind the curve when it comes to adoption among the wider team across the enterprise

- Seemingly in a constant state of design/redesign/implementation for new systems

- Usually over budget in technology, and challenged with finding consistent measurability across a longer time frame.

To address these challenges and enable new engagement strategies, we need a new technology model for marketing teams. This new model of enterprise marketing technology provides scalability and sustainability, as well as the agility required for today's constantly changing landscape.

NEW MARKETING TECHNOLOGY MODEL: BUILT TO CHANGE

In his paper "Systems of Engagement and the Future of Enterprise IT," Geoffrey Moore explains that we are in a "new era of IT." According to Moore, the old "systems of record" (the large backbone IT systems) are now being supplemented and extended by "systems of engagement" solutions that are built to facilitate communication and collaboration. In describing the importance of this "sea change," Moore says:

> *"Amidst the texting and Twittering and Facebooking of a generation of digital natives, the fundamentals of next-generation communication*

and collaboration are being worked out. For them it is clear, there is no going back. So, at a minimum, if you expect these folks to be your customers, your employees, and your citizens . . . then you need to apply THEIR expectations to the next generation of enterprise IT systems. "[85]

Moore specifically analyzes content management and business intelligence applications and points out that the focus must be "*on empowering the middle of the enterprise to communicate and collaborate across business boundaries, global time zones, and language and cultural barriers, using next-generation IT applications and infrastructure adapted from the consumer space.*"

Moore is certainly right about the needed changes. But, he takes a long-term view of the transformation. Today, the requirement for marketing to adapt immediately means that this new technology adoption model must be adjusted quickly for the new and evolving realities.

THE NEW EXPERIENCES TECHNOLOGY STACK: A BACKBONE WITH ROOM TO FLEX

A new model to facilitate a seventh era of marketing—one that will empower marketers to create powerful digital content experiences—is starting to emerge from a few forward-looking technology vendors. This new model accommodates the need of large enterprises to scale and provide consistent experiences across a large employee base that adapts to the conversational, flexible, and chaotic nature of today's marketing organization.

One vendor offering a suite of products can deliver this model or multiple vendors' products can be integrated seamlessly. The key is that this marketing technology stack approach can be optimized for today's content marketing and engagement processes.

The stack is comprised of three discrete layers that, at the lower end, are made up of systems of record and become systems of engagement as they move closer to the customer on the front end. In every case, they must be flexible and interchangeable.

This is not a physical architecture of a specific technology solution, but rather a model that marketers can use to begin developing their business requirements for the technology solutions they require.

The layers are:

- **Core data management**. This is the lowest layer—the foundation and storage of customer, content, and transactional data; it serves the global enterprise. It is supported by large databases and closely adheres to standards so that data can be easily extracted and used. Whether cloud-based or closely held within the organization, it should enable information as a service.

- **Engagement management**. This middle layer of technology should be able to interface with anything above and below it. It provides the interface into, and out of, the core data management layer and provides optimization based on business rules that can be applied to display content contextually.

- **Content channel and experience management**. This top layer should be as flexible, portable, and/or disposable as any media strategy used to be. Content channels such as YouTube, Facebook, or blogs are the marketer's new "media buy." They are important only so long as they are useful. This layer will be constantly changing and morphing, so it should aim for zero-friction in order to add or dispose of elements easily.

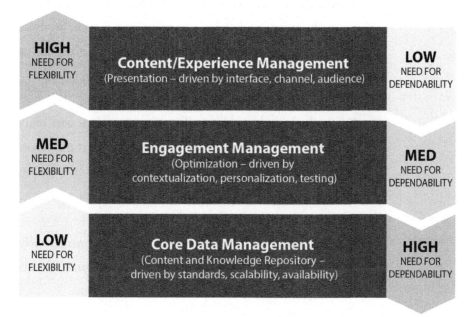

The three layers of the experience technology stack can help align marketing and technology strategies, providing high-level goals for each kind of technology to use to build experiences.

Here's an example of this experience technology model:

- A large consumer hotel company has restructured the management of its websites for web experience management.

    o With more than 600 websites to manage across multiple devices, the company has deployed a solid backbone for web content management and measurement.

    o The company uses an enterprise-wide web content management solution with integrated analytics to deliver everything in a standardized format to hotel staff—from web visitor information to brand marketers to per-hotel revenue information.

o This standardized content store gives them the flexibility to easily create and deliver content across web, mobile, and social channels—and remain more nimble across numerous social media.

o By deploying channel-specific strategies, they can react quickly and conversationally to consumers that may have issues while on the property, and store that information globally.

o Recent "wins" include having the ability to immediately provide a guest with a free breakfast after the guest Tweets that there was a problem with his or her room.

CCM MEETS TECHNOLOGY ADOPTION: BUILT TO ADAPT

One of the biggest dangers for enterprise marketing groups today is the temptation to repeat the mistakes made during "Web 1.0." Just as the "ebusiness team" was often separated from the core business in the late 1990s, so, too, are social and web experience teams often isolated from both corporate marketing and IT today.

CCM and the function of delivering rich digital experiences across any channel require that these teams collaborate on one cohesive strategy. As a result, the experience management technologies facilitating those processes can converge effectively to integrate and manage all three layers: core data management, engagement management, and content channel and experience management.

This new adaptive system will be staffed by flexible teams who also will be challenged to change and rearrange as new strategies are deployed by the enterprise. These de-siloed teams should ultimately work together in the marketing department to generate a phenomenon that scientists call "emergence," where relatively simple and separate interactions develop into productive patterns. Then, the whole ultimately becomes much greater than the sum of its parts.

Tomorrow's marketing and communications teams will succeed by learning to adapt—and by deploying systems of engagement that facilitate adaption. By building to change, the marketing department builds to succeed.

WHAT'S NEXT: THE 90-DAY VISION

The First Month—Alignment with technology

- Look for ways to get insight from the technology leaders into their roadmap and build collaborative strategies. Seek to develop a strategy that enhances the technologist's ability to determine "how" a particular technology should function, and the marketer's ability to determine "what" process it should facilitate. A common ground might be found in viewing a simple agenda to agree on categories of:

  o Engagement and relationship—work to create fast and agile ways to facilitate new platforms and quickly iterate ideas with the technology and marketing team. Basically, the CMO needs to understand this process intimately and be able to quickly communicate the fast-changing iterations that may be required.

o Intelligence and insight—the CMO and CIO need to collaborate on a methodology that is focused on learning—drawing value out of what actually happened vs. siloed push-and-pull of data. The CMO and CIO need to work hand-in-hand here.

o Shared values and exceeded expectations—the CMO and CIO must go beyond merely understanding one another's agenda; they need to collaborate on a joined strategy where a partnership is critical to the business.

- Create that joined strategy by viewing the technologists as core team members who help to manage the portfolio of experiences— or at least as a support layer that will be informed of all the story maps being created.

The Second Month—The technology stack and new technology acquisition

- Getting alignment on a technology stack and purchase strategy for customer-driven experiences can be difficult. One way to focus your efforts is to look at audience development for content-driven experiences as the goal. With that in mind, and in conjunction with your technology team, look to an approach across three layers:

o Core data management—driven by the technologists and acknowledge that, once set, it will not change often.

o Engagement management—as a middle layer of technology that interfaces with data, changes here are considered and infrequent. Business rules will feed the data collection.

○ Content and experience management—a top layer that should be as flexible and/or disposable as any media strategy. Here the changes will come fast and furious, and experimentation will be high. Once set into a core strategy—or once value has been proven by a particular experience—then perhaps it becomes more of an engagement management approach.

The Third Month and Onward—Technology enablement as a core piece of CCM

• Technology will certainly affect the CCM portfolio management strategy. Delivering rich digital experiences across many channels will require ongoing collaboration on one cohesive strategy. Experience management technologies can converge effectively to integrate and manage all three technology layers. Conduct technology reviews as part of the ongoing CCM agenda.

ENDNOTES

84   "Google brings agile to agencies with 'Agile Creativity' vision." Chief Marketing Technologist, August 9, 2012. Available at: http://www.chiefmartec.com/

85   "Systems of Engagement and the Future of Enterprise IT: A Sea Change in Enterprise IT," by Geoffrey Moore. Available at: http://www.aiim.org/futurehistory/

chapter 10:
MEASURING FOR MEANING INSTEAD OF MEDIOCRITY

"Tell me how you measure me and I will tell you how I will behave. If you measure me in an illogical way…do not complain about illogical behavior." | Eliyahu Goldratt

Before you get too excited, you need to know that this is not a book about marketing measurement. There, whew, we said it.

There are innumerable experts in the field of data measurement who derive actionable insight out of the ways that marketing and advertising are measured. As we have indicated, we are focused on putting function before form, story before expression, and meaning before action.

That said, we can safely say that measurement—especially as it pertains to content and experience-driven marketing—is in a world of hurt. The stark perception that content-driven marketing cannot be measured (as opposed to the actual results) is the most often cited reason that content marketing initiatives are cancelled.

Therefore, as we move into the new era of Experiences—as we "lean in" with our capital "M"—we must CHANGE how we approach the very idea of what measurement means.

This chapter is about changing our *approach* to measurement.

MARKETERS ARE WIRED TO GET MEASUREMENT WRONG

In 2008, science historian Michael Shermer coined the word "patternicity." In his book *The Believing Brain*, he defines it as "the tendency to find meaningful patterns in both meaningful and meaningless noise."[86] Shermer says that humans have the tendency to "infuse the patterns with meaning, intention, and agency." He calls this latter tendency "agenticity."

So, as humans, we're wired to make two types of errors that have relevance here:

- Type 1 Errors – the false positive, or the pattern that doesn't really exist

- Type 2 Errors – the false negative, where we fail to see the real pattern that actually does exist.

As marketers, we are even MORE hardwired for not only making Type 1 errors, but for the "agenticity" that goes along with doing so.

One of the disadvantages that analytics technology has brought is in its promise to reduce all marketing down to an algorithm. The ability to be "data-driven" has pressured marketers into analytics as "proof of life" for every creative strategy the team puts forward. Thus, the team is trained to see successful patterns in ANYTHING that even resembles success.

Web analytics dashboards—churning through "small data"—are billboards for Type 1 Errors. More traffic? The light is green. Never mind that the reason we have more traffic is because something we've just published went viral in a bad way. Fast food restaurant Chick-fil-A's web traffic quadrupled over the span of one month in 2012 during the controversy over their CEO's comments on the LGBT community. Is that a good thing?

How about more "time on site"? As marketers, we interpret this as visitors are more engaged with our content, not that they may be having difficulty finding what they are looking for.

We see more "likes" as an indicator of success on Facebook, without even acknowledging that people actually have to "like" your page before they can comment on how much they hate you.

A "data-driven marketing" mindset has pushed many marketers into scrambling to find patterns of success that may or may not be there. This tunnel vision has marketers using data in narrow ways. This is addressed in an IBM paper titled, "From Stretched to Strengthened," which reports on study findings that most CMOs use data to optimize transactions, as opposed to using it to glean insights to deepen their relationships with customers.[87]

In an interview with the authors, Gordon Evans, senior director of product marketing for SalesForce.com's Marketing Cloud, framed this disconnect by saying:

> "There's this whole notion of being able to identify and convert people in a different kind of funnel—where you take them from strangers, to friends, to fans to advocates. The way that's done is through engagement-focused experiences."

Put simply, marketers have to stop looking at analytics as *only* a means to improve converting calls-to-action and as "proof-of-life" that a campaign was worth paying for. Instead, they must also start to look for meaning, using content and data to deepen the engagement and to improve the process of creating engagement-focused experiences.

WHAT DO ANALYTICS MEAN TO MARKETING?

If you look up the definition of "analytics" in the dictionary, you'll find:

ANALYTICS

/Anl'itiks /

noun

plural noun: analytics

1. The systematic computational analysis of data or statistics.

2. Information resulting from the systematic analysis of data or statistics.

Two things stand out to us in that definition. Nowhere do we see the words insight, improvement, or actionable. In other words, it's the systematic reporting of the patterns of data that has been captured. In fact, that's exactly what the IBM study found.

But let's be honest—this is really the definition of what analytics has become for marketers:

ANALYTICS (The marketers' version)

/Anl'itiks /

noun

plural noun: analytics

1. The systematic computational method of making data say anything that justifies our actions.

2. Information manipulated to ensure that marketing or other departments illustrate "proof of life" to justify their existence.

3. Weapon of mass delusion.

That's right. Delusional. This is where we are with measurement. We are right where physicist and business management thought leader Eli Goldratt said we would be. Our companies use increasing amounts of technology to define how marketing should be measured. And we, as marketers, respond accordingly with our behavior. Because we are measured in increasingly illogical ways, we start behaving just as illogically.

As an extreme example of this, we worked with a large technical infrastructure company. Their customer email database had 175,000 addresses. They invested hundreds of thousands of dollars in an email technology solution that would actually send that many emails on a weekly basis. Each time they would send an email, half of them (85,000) would bounce back as undeliverable. This was because the database was never maintained or pruned.

When we asked the marketing team why they didn't just prune the database, and delete the 85,000 that were bouncing each time, they told us "because if management sees that our email subscription rate dropped by 50% they would cut our budget for email."

Yes ... that's delusional.

THE MEASUREMENT PYRAMID

In *Managing Content Marketing*, Robert Rose and Joe Pulizzi presented the measurement pyramid, a new approach for the process of measuring content marketing. The pyramid is comprised of three key levels of analytics that inform the process of creating content for business purposes:

1. Primary indicators: Goals—which indicate progress toward a desired achievement. These are the numbers we actually report on.

2. Secondary indicators: Key performance indicators (KPIs)— secondary goals and indicators toward the progress of the goals. These are integrated measurements of content that help us improve the process toward meeting our primary goals.

3. User indicators: Data points—data we collect that helps us on a day-to-day basis inform the process to alter course toward our goal.

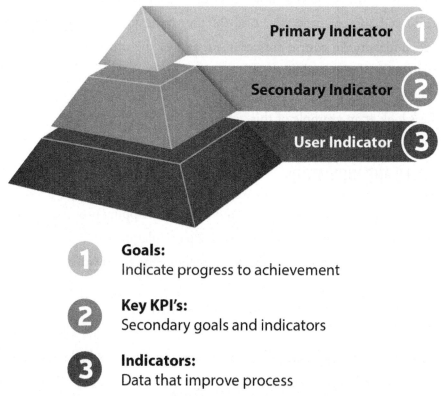

Primary Indicator ①

Secondary Indicator ②

User Indicator ③

① Goals:
Indicate progress to achievement

② Key KPI's:
Secondary goals and indicators

③ Indicators:
Data that improve process

The measurement pyramid is designed to help segment the KPIs that help improve process vs. those that we should be reporting as part of our goals.

As a CCM governing process begins to take root, the measurement pyramid can be used to elevate and integrate measurement beyond a myopic focus on ensuring that every graph goes up and to the right. It can be a framework that lets us start to measure the efficacy of *content* across a multi-channel strategy and provide an incentive for cross-functional teams to align their goals. This approach can help marketers report the MEANING of numbers; it offers the insight necessary to develop more delightful experiences, as opposed to being a scorecard that helps record marketing team performance.

The key is in the reporting.

As a strategic function, marketing should report *only* the primary indicators. The secondary indicators exist to help improve the marketing team and content processes. And the user indicators exist only to help individuals make course corrections that fuel the achievements within their areas of responsibility.

Let's look at an example of this.

GOALS AND INDICATORS

As we remember from Chapter 8 and the story mapping process, we may have a number of goals associated with a particular initiative. One way to think about goals is to state them in the following framework:

OBJECTIVE + TIME FRAME + CONSTRAINT

At first, establishing a constraint may seem like a bit of a ball and chain; however, these three parameters are important because they allow us to be more creative while striving to reach our goals. In short, we have three levers to pull and push. Thus, we can be more precise than just saying the goal for a content marketing initiative is to *"increase qualified leads by 10%."*

Instead, we can be quite specific. For example, we can set a goal for a content-driven experience that says:

> *Increase qualified leads by 10% in six months with only a 5% budget increase.*

Using the measurement pyramid, we might come up with the following tiers of measurement:

GOAL	Increase qualified leads by 10% in six months with a 5% budget increase
PRIMARY INDICATORS	• # of qualified leads • Cost
SECONDARY INDICATORS (examples)	• Unqualified leads • Cost per lead (CPL) • Blog subscribers • Email subscribers • Downloads • Webinar attendees • Website visitors
USER INDICATORS (examples)	• Likes/followers • A/B test results • Cost per visitor (CPV) • Video views • Webinar registrants

The example above is simply meant to be illustrative. As you might expect, those lists on the secondary indicators and user indicators could get quite long depending on the number of goals, as well as the amount of data that you're tracking. And, yes, you probably have more than one goal that you're trying to reach.

But you can now see how this pyramid might tier within different functional groups. For example, the sales enablement team will have goals that drive qualified leads, whereas the field marketing team may have goals that drive awareness and initial downloads of content. The product marketing team may have sales revenue goals for new products. These individual goals can share integrated secondary indicators—and then the individual managers can share user indicators. The shape may resemble this:

Shared Goals:
Indicate progress to achievment

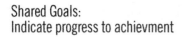 Goals  Goals

Key KPI's:
Collaborative Goals

Indicators:
Data that improve
all processes

The measurement pyramid can scale to different groups with cross-functioning goals. User indicators become a pool for the team to draw from to understand how to improve toward the goals.

Ultimately, the application of a measurement methodology is what's important. The measurement pyramid is one idea. But, the true goal should be to de-silo the measurement so that different groups don't ostensibly compete with one another.

In one example of this, we worked with a consumer-facing insurance company. Like many B2C companies, they had different silos of marketing teams working on different parts of the marketing strategy. When they decided to launch a blog as a content-driven experience initiative, things got complicated. That's when they began to understand the challenges with siloed measurement.

Once the project was ready to launch, the content team went to the web marketing team and asked for a prominent button on the front page of the website. The web marketing team said "no," because they were measured on traffic. Therefore, anything that took away from their traffic numbers would hurt their success. The then disheartened content team went to the social team to ask if they would distribute their blog posts to the social channels (especially Facebook where they had more than a million likes). The social team said "no," because they were measured on "engagement." When they posted cute pictures of cats, they got 1,000 or more likes. When they posted anything having to do with insurance, they got fewer than 10 likes.

This is a classic example of Goldratt's theory. These teams had altered their behavior to meet illogical measurement. They were actually competing for the attention of their own consumers.

THE MANAGERS OF MEANING

The measurement pyramid won't solve all of the marketing measurement challenges—but it does come with a number of benefits:

- It places the primary focus on measuring what's important, and more importantly, what's meaningful: progress toward a business goal.

- If we can avoid reporting secondary indicators, it frees teams from an "always up and to the right" mentality. Innovative new experiences that may actually reduce traffic to a particular channel (or migrate it away from some other platform) can survive because the team isn't afraid to lose the incremental success to that channel.

- It can prevent departmental competition. Measuring the content, NOT the team producing it, can provide a tremendous amount of benefit. When we are free to use the user indicators to help us improve our job, and the secondary indicators to help the cross-functional teams reach the goals, then we have every incentive to experiment without fear of failure.

For big data to have any value beyond existing information, marketers must move beyond using analytics as a method to prove success or ROI. Instead, they must use data and measurement as a method to improve the continuing process from which we derive more meaningful insight and develop more delightful customer experiences.

Like innovation itself, companies have been talking about this changed process for many years. But, now, as we move into a new era of marketing, *we really need to do it.*

We will most likely need to add new roles to our teams (ones that typically don't exist yet in most corporations). Only then will we be equipped to peel back the layers of big data and make them smaller and more integrated with our business. These new players aren't necessarily the data scientists or mathematicians that have been all the buzz of late (although those roles are important for different reasons). Rather, these people will have a talent for asking questions about the data, our customers, and influencers. They will be skilled at listening, conversing, synthesizing, and transforming facts and results into meaningful insights.

We call these people the "managers of meaning."

CONTENT EXPERIENCE MEASUREMENT

Although this is not a chapter on measurement, there is a way that secondary indicators can be integrated into the CCM process. As we stated in Chapter 6, one of the core responsibilities of the CCM team is to measure both the individual experiences the company creates, as well as the portfolio of all the experiences together.

To this end, we have created a framework for content marketing measurement across three specific categories. When layered into the secondary indicators of the measurement pyramid, this framework provides a nicely integrated way to specifically measure content marketing efforts.

The three categories are:

- **Attention Metrics**

  Attention metrics measure audience development. Part of the reason we create content-driven experiences is to aggregate an audience (independent of their stage of engagement with our company) and measure whether we are creating value to that audience. Here we measure how content consumption and content brand awareness is building that audience. In other words, how are we broadening the awareness of our solution and our approach to solving customers' problems and wants with content? Examples of what to measure include:

    o Blog subscribers (especially those subscribed via email)

    o White paper downloads

    o Regular webinar attendees

    o Content marketing database growth across multiple platforms

    o Attendees at physical events

o Customers subscribed to our content-driven loyalty program.

- **Social Metrics**

Social metrics identify audience and conversation influence. In other words, as part of creating value that is separate from our product and service, we want to measure how our content is being shared, and how much of that is turning into conversation. We need to ask how our content is influencing the larger discussion about the approach or sentiment we're trying to create. One of our biggest challenges with turning our businesses into media companies is getting our approach, our way of telling our story, widely shared.

Remember, as we said at the beginning of this book, we won't have the capacity to be on every single social channel that exists now and in the future. Every time our content resonates to the point that people want to share it willingly across social channels, reduces the time we must spend to BE on that channel. We should be measuring this to determine whether our content-driven experience is creating value. Examples include:

o Social listening mentions and shares—not of our brand per se, but of the experiences we're creating through our strategy.

o Growth of our social networks as it applies to our content-driven experiences (e.g., comments, interactions, and, yes, engagement).

o Sentiment analysis—again, not necessarily of our brand or products, but of the new conversations and key concepts we're driving into the zeitgeist. (Look at what HubSpot has been able to achieve by focusing the conversation on the term "inbound marketing." They've ostensibly created an entire marketing category simply by creating amazing content that fueled that conversation.)

- **Effectiveness Metrics**

Effectiveness metrics identify how well the content is living up to its purpose. The goal when we develop content-driven experiences is to change or enhance some type of customer behavior. This is a measurement of how the experience is measuring up to that goal. This is where we assess the platform's contribution to the business. Examples include:

o Number of qualified leads from the blog

o Increase in loyalty of customers signed up to the magazine

o Shopping cart value of those engaged with content experiences

o Net Promoter Score increase from loyalty magazine subscribers.

PUTTING IT TOGETHER WITH THE PYRAMID

Again, with the above, we are not identifying ALL marketing metrics, but rather those that are associated with developing experiences and content marketing as a process. Ultimately this is a layer, an approach that gets infused into the overall marketing strategy.

As you begin to measure experiences, you look at your *user indicators*, and then at your team-oriented *secondary indicators*. As shown in the example chart below, you can map different metrics into both (and, if appropriate, even your primary goals), across the categories of attention, social, and effectiveness. This will give you a picture of how you are working and how an experience is helping the marketing program.

	Attention Metrics (audience development)	Social Metrics (conversation influence)	Effectiveness Metrics (effectiveness)
USER INDICATORS	• Impressions • Page views • Downloads	• Retweets, likes, +1's • Forwards • Inbound links	• Blog visitors • Time on site • Referral traffic
SECONDARY INDICATORS	• Share of voice • Audience/marketing database growth • White paper downloads	• Social shares • Sentiment analysis • Influencer mentions	• Cost per visitor or lead • Blog subscribers • New leads

Perhaps individuals or teams within the CCM take a "box" (rather than a channel), thus making their group responsible for a category of measurement rather than a siloed channel. For example, let's say the company's new content-driven experience is a thought leadership blog. So, if a team is now responsible for attention metrics that are secondary indicators, they might be responsible for:

• Blog subscriber growth

• Email response rates from subscribers

- SEO metrics

- Conversions from PR efforts to promote the blog

- Social traffic to blog posts.

In short, the team is now responsible for "audience development" instead of a channel.

ADJUST, MONITOR, AND ITERATE THE PROCESS

This is the evolution. Because instead of being "data driven," we can now be "data inspired"—eager to explore new ways to make our content experiences successful.

We're no longer wrapped around the axles of the number of visitors, email subscribers, and followers. We're actually focusing on what's important to meet our goals—and everybody is collaborating on those goals. This helps us define what ROI really means.

Content-driven experiences are not managed separately, but rather as an integrated piece of your marketing strategy. For example, you don't manage things like "how many leads did the telephone produce?" Or, is the "telephone" a viable channel for us? You just don't do that. It's part of a whole program.

In the same way, content is part of an entire program. But, you can and should examine its contribution and how you might improve it. The investment should be easy enough to calculate. The contribution can flow from a number of things. For example, it can come through the

KPIs you review, or it can show how you successfully contribute overall to the marketing goal.

A completely viable primary indicator for a blog may only be to provide more traffic into the main website because that's top of the funnel for the sales process. That may be its *only goal*. If it accomplishes that, and its cost is requisite with that accomplishment, that's a perfectly laudable business goal.

Everything does not have to deliver sales directly. We can start to ask better questions, such as, *"Does the content really create a more valuable customer? Are we getting more engaged traffic? Are we getting more inbound links? Are we able to better cross-sell to our existing customers? Are our customers more loyal?"*

Those are all valuable. In fact, we should be asking our "managers of meaning" those very questions if we're ever going to expand beyond content as just a lead generator. Instead, we should expect it to create value for the business.

WHAT'S NEXT: THE 90-DAY VISION

The First Month

- Can you change the culture of measurement in your organization? Can you realign your measurement strategy in marketing more broadly? Or should you take a more incremental step?

- Assuming the latter, spend time creating the measurement map for a content experience across the different layers of attention, social, and effectiveness metrics. Map these into a pyramid.

- Experiment with creating teams that will manage elements of that measurement map, as opposed to channels. Does this process work cross-functionally? Is it better?

The Second Month

- Are there more meaningful ways you can measure your content-driven experiences other than "more visitors" or "more sales"? Consider looking at things like "deeper insight into personas," "cost-savings in third-party research," or "ways to develop better programmatic advertising" as important business goals rather than the obvious.

- Look to integrate these more meaningful ways to measure into existing content experiences. What would that look like? How would it change the direction of specific content-driven experiences?

The Third Month and Onward

- Identify your "manager of meaning." Can you find someone within the organization who can start to use data and measurement as a competitive advantage and feed that insight into the creation of content-driven experiences? Should you hire outside for this?

ENDNOTES

86   http://en.wikipedia.org/wiki/Michael_Shermer

87   http://www-01.ibm.com/common/ssi/cgi-bin/
     ssialias?subtype=XB&infotype=PM&appname=GBSE_GB_TI_
     USEN&htmlfid=GBE03433USEN&attachment=GBE03433USEN.PDF

conclusion:
BUILDING LIQUID PROCESSES

"Success is not owned; it's leased, and rent is due
every day!" | J.J. Watt

We started this book with a simple question: What do you *really* do?

We hope that by now, if the answer isn't clear, there is at least a path forward for you to answer it.

If we're perfectly honest, we care much less about the companies you work for—and much more about you. Now, we certainly hope that you're able to take some, or all, of the better practices we've outlined in this book and put them to work in your business. We want you to be the rock star in your organization and the change agent who moves it forward. We hope that you're able to evolve your company's marketing strategy into the differentiating, strategic function that it deserves to be. We do hope your business can change and evolve into the new era of marketing by developing new processes to get there. But more importantly:

We hope *you* can change.

As you might have noticed, we're big fans of Peter Drucker. And we can't resist adding one more quote of his in here:

"Culture eats strategy for breakfast."

After you read a business book or attend a conference, you usually go back and reflect on the positive things you got out of it; maybe you take note of some of the things you disagreed with. However, more often than not, you'll set aside all of the changes it suggests.

It's one thing to actually answer the question, "What do you *really* do?" It's another thing to actually go do it.

It's *you* who will be successful in transforming your business. It's *you* who will pass this book on to your peers, your boss, or your team to help them understand how to make these changes. It's *you* who will lean in, step up, and transform some of these "better practices" into BEST practices.

We've covered a lot of marketing and content ground in this book. We realize that much of the process of the creation of CCM, story mapping, and a new paradigm of measurement—all set in the context of making marketing more strategic—can be overwhelming.

We hope this book becomes tattered if you bought the print version. Or, if it's digital, we hope it's one of those eBooks that has tons of highlighted passages, saved notes, and remains in the upper left corner of the first screen on your tablet reader. We hope that some, or all, of the processes add value to your unique approach to creating content-driven experiences. Most of all, we hope this book can be a periodic check-in to help you sustain success.

The road ahead will be full of challenging adventure and will require YOU to be fluid and adaptive to meet those challenges. Here are a few things we hope you take with you.

CONTEXTUALIZE THE APPROACH OF CCM

The double-edged sword of a great marketing strategy is that it is, on one side, new and uncrowded; on the other, there is no template. When we get asked about templates for content-driven experiences, we ask back: "Would you really want one if it existed?" Is that what you want for your career? To color in the lines that someone else has drawn?

That said, take some of what we talked about in Chapters 2 and 3 and contextualize it within your business. If you're a senior executive, you need to foster a culture of innovation and strategy within marketing.

If you're a junior or entry-level manager, start thinking of ways to carve out time to create innovative methods to take to your boss.

- Where can you start to build collaborative networks within your business?

- Where can you begin to delegate the tasks that simply describe the value of your business?

- How can you start to carve out a position that creates innovative value in your company?

Marketing truly has the opportunity to be the differentiating force within the business.

Take, for example, Kraft's Julie Fleischer, our Chapter 6 hero. When she was challenged with a potential dead end in managing a print magazine in which the company saw a future, Fleischer transformed the entire print magazine strategy into an innovative process that created exponential value for her company.

CLASSIC LINEAR AND HIERARCHICAL STRUCTURES WILL BE INADEQUATE

Legacy systems that focus on campaigns and promotions have marketers geared toward seeing their work in a linear fashion through to completion, or toward abandoning it completely if things are headed in the wrong direction. McKinsey & Company points out that the areas outside of marketing are also locked into models that focus on products and services rather than aligning with changing customer dynamics.[88]

Earlier, we talked about the ability of marketers to organize for agility, not speed. When we talk about building liquid processes, what we mean is the ability for marketers to create processes that respond to the demands of a fast-changing digital world in which customers change even faster. Marketing leaders must establish processes that remove the barriers that impede business. Instead, they must enable agility across all departments in order to create the experiences that matter to target audiences in the most critical moments.

It's hard to find familiarity and points of reference in a world that has no "normal." In order to transform organizations, marketers must remain flexible and agile as they adopt new business strategies, work across departments, and lead diverse teams.

It's easy for us to say "be more agile." But, what does that actually look like? In a report by the Center for Creative Leadership, authors Adam Mitchinson and Robert Morris warn that the behaviors that are effective in one level of the organization don't necessarily translate into other levels. They point out that agile leaders are better equipped to use new strategies and to lead change within their organizations. Here are the six leadership characteristics that Mitchinson and Morris say are most important for success:

1. **The courage to challenge the status quo.** Speaking up and openly questioning how things have always been done can prove daunting. By questioning long-held beliefs and working to break down silos between groups, content marketers will discover new and innovative ways to look at challenges and creatively solve them. The more diverse your experiences, the broader the perspectives you bring to your role and the more capable you will be of delving deeper to find new ways to meet your goals across the enterprise.

2. **The ability to remain calm in the midst of adversity.** Agile learners draw on past experiences to remain present and engaged when they face ambiguous and/or high-pressure situations. This allows them to tap into more insightful thinking processes—even at times when inspiration may be at its lowest.

3. **Taking time for reflection.** In the midst of all the demands placed on us and on our teams, agile leaders manage to take time to step back and reflect on the work we do, the meaning we create, and how that meaning affects our customers' experiences. Having new experiences doesn't guarantee that you'll learn from them; however, reflecting upon them can offer deeper insights into how you will perform, how you will work with others, and how you will approach new challenges.

4. **Purposely seeking challenging situations.** Comfort and growth can't coexist. Agile learners understand the need to push themselves and their abilities—and to explore situations where there is no proven process or outcome. Marketers who prioritize continuous learning will come to understand the ways that risk can lead to opportunity.

5. **Being open to learning.** Breaking down legacy thinking is the first step to opening your mind to new possibilities. Instead of relying on the crutch of "best" practices, think "next" practices. Don't let the way you've always done things—even if it's brought you success—circumvent the pathways to new ideas and experiences.

6. **Avoiding defensive thinking.** Openness is fundamental to increasing knowledge. But openness isn't a one-way process; it requires talking about what you believe and why you believe it, as well as initiating honest, heart-to-heart conversations that may make you feel vulnerable. When you share your ideas, people will probably give you feedback, and some may disagree with your approach. But, agile learners resist the urge to become defensive. Instead, they listen carefully and seek to understand others' points

of view and perspectives. This is how they learn valuable lessons and insights that may come in handy for future challenges.[89]

BEWARE OF THE GLADIATOR EFFECT: IT'S NOT ALL OR NOTHING

Many organizations follow an all-or-nothing approach to new ideas. Teams research, put together plans, back them up with data, and present them to the person(s) in charge of that area...and wait for approval. "Approval" usually comes in the form of a thumbs up or thumbs down— just like the Roman people gave the gladiators. There's no opportunity for on-going collaboration, development, or refinement. Either the idea lives or dies; the outcome is black or white.

Unfortunately, that approach doesn't lend itself to evolving ideas or to taking the best parts and pieces from good ideas and making them great ideas. Instead, it sets teams up to look for approval from authorities who may or may not be the best judge of what creates a valuable customer experience. Many times, the managers making the live-or-die decisions have little to no contact with customers. So, they are out of touch with the changing dynamics of the marketplace.

This is why small, nimble startups sideswipe big companies with big budgets. The Goliaths are bogged down with groupthink and cannot appreciate collaborative decision making. Big budgets give people a false sense of security even though bigger doesn't mean smarter or more innovative.

People like control because they think it helps them know what to expect. But you can't control an uncontrollable environment. Whether or not companies are immediately successful with agile marketing, marketers need to get comfortable with a more fluid process. Teams think that projects fail because they are poorly managed; however, it's more often the case that what's needed has changed during the process—and they couldn't recognize and embrace the change and adjust along the way. Failure ensues when managers focus on controlling events instead of guiding a process and empowering teams to use a framework that allows for change and then helping them clear the path to make those changes happen.

UNDERSTAND THAT INNOVATION IS A PROCESS, NOT AN INVENTION

Company culture confuses people about the real nature of innovation. Inventions are what you sell. But, innovation is about new ways to do business with your customers. In today's world, innovation is more about new business models than new products (inventions).

The classic innovation example is Apple. They didn't invent the phone, the music player, or online music downloads. But they developed a business model that put them all together and has exploded into a $170 billion enterprise.[90]

When Apple launched iTunes in 2003, they sold 1 million songs in the first week.[91] The iTunes app store isn't particularly sophisticated; the parts and pieces that make up the online store existed before Apple came along. Apple's innovation contribution is how they put the pieces together to create a platform that distributes content to millions of customers. Apple created a radical new business model that found a better way to create value by improving the delivery of music that customers wanted.

Improving customer outcomes requires marketing to lead the transition toward more organic processes. Marketers are uniquely positioned to understand customer problems and how to improve outcomes. *"What is the customer struggling with and what can I offer?"* is a very different mindset from, *"What can I build and sell?"*

To transform business, we must build a culture of low politics and high transparency. We must think more like innovative entrepreneurs who embrace new thinking, customer involvement, early testing, and collaborative decision making. We must then make sure that our work delivers valuable customer experiences.

In his book *The Lean Startup*, author Eric Ries talks about how companies need to learn, iterate, and deliver outcomes in new ways. To do this, business (even marketing) functions require an approach to guide their work that is just as rigorous as that of engineers and product developers.

The lean approach means that marketers need to release themselves from their paralyzing fear of failure and move into an entrepreneurial risk-acceptance mindset. Entrepreneurs and startups recognize that to vet new ideas that offer the best chance of success, you have to talk to customers in order to understand the subtle differences between what they need and what you sell.[92]

Ries indicates that startups must have a "true north" for what they want and where they're headed so they can end up with the right product.

For marketers, when we think in terms of experiences rather than products, we must use the same entrepreneurial, lean startup approach to bringing change to our organizations. We're not looking to instill another process that creates more meetings and bogs things down with more bureaucracy. Rather, we're looking for just enough process to keep teams nimble as we scale our content operations. That doesn't free us from bureaucracy, however. If anything, our roles are even more important because it's our responsibility to break down barriers within the organization.

MAKE THE AUDIENCES AND ARCHETYPES YOUR OWN

One of Julie Fleischer's innovations at Kraft (as part of her content-purpose strategy) was to segment her content by time and quality. She knew she'd have content that was ephemeral and low-production. She understood she'd have content that needed to be high-production value and evergreen. In segmenting this strategy—and in working hard to understand what her audiences wanted—Fleischer could assign each of these purposes to individual teams, from agencies to her own internal marketing group.

In the same way, as you come out of Chapters 4 and 5, you can create your own methodologies for identifying new audiences, develop your own archetypes, or layer on to the ones we've created. The archetypes we discuss in Chapter 5 are meant to provide a baseline of why creating content for a specific purpose changes with the purpose of the platform.

THE ONLY DIFFERENCE BETWEEN A RUT AND A GRAVE IS DEPTH

In Chapter 2, we discussed the need for marketers to take on roles as growth drivers, unifiers, and innovators. Your vision—your WHY—will serve as your north star and guide you and your teams toward a long-term common goal.

This also will be your most frustrating effort.

People love familiarity, even in uncomfortable circumstances. A known evil almost always trumps the unknown, even if the odds show that change can improve results dramatically by delivering:

- Better experiences for customers

- More opportunities for creativity in your work

- Greater collaboration in solving problems.

All companies struggle to infuse an understanding throughout their organization of strategy and how to execute on it. What varies is the level of difficulty of that struggle. Best-in-class companies do a much better job of communicating how every employee needs to learn, iterate, and evaluate as part of the larger organization doing the same. Marketers need to take the lead in infusing strategy across the enterprise, so that when course pivots need to be made, employees are more willing to change. This is where decisions get really difficult. Legacy thinking and the reluctance to change behavior leads us to treat strategies as if they're cast in stone rather than being continually adjustable.

"Wait, I thought we had a strategy. Why are we changing it...again?!"

Every marketer detests hearing that phrase. There's a difference between changing a strategy and evolving a strategy. The former means that it wasn't the right strategy to start with. The latter means that you understand that as you execute, conditions change, and you need to pivot along the way to stay relevant.

In Chapter 7, when we talk about story mapping, it's the journey part of the process where we continually ask:

- How are we doing compared with the outcomes we sought?

- What, if any, of our original assumptions do we need to change?

Teams can get stuck in groupthink, paralyzed by looking "wrong" because they adjusted (pivoted) mid-strategy. But those that do are more likely to embrace innovation and be able to create and iterate faster. The point to keep in mind is: always focus on the unique, content-driven experiences that you want to create for your audiences. The experiences that you create are the end results of your strategy. That's what will keep your content fresh and enticing for your audiences and make them *want* to keep coming back. And it's what will transition marketers out of the campaign mentality and into true content marketing.

AGILITY AND SCALE ARE NOT OXYMORONS

"Agility" and "enterprise" can indeed work together. As large companies consider how they can become more innovative and instill this mindset across the organization, they understand that size and scale can be their biggest hurdle unless they change the way they think.

Enterprises that welcome the opportunity for open collaboration realize that agility is a competitive advantage. And marketing is the logical driver of this change. As we covered in Chapter 2, marketing's role *needs* to evolve and expand in order to guide our companies where they need to go. Marketers can best understand where industries are going and what customers want—and then translate that into practical action.

We marketers can examine strategies to understand where and when to pivot, and how those pivots work across multiple, interconnected teams.

GE is a perfect example. When the company decided to implement the Lean Startup philosophy as part of its "simplification" push after the financial crisis a few years ago, it was marketers who often served as project managers. Dubbed FastWorks, GE's version of lean wasn't about corporate restructuring; it was about transforming how they did business in order to develop better outcomes for customers more quickly.

By giving teams more autonomy and encouraging them to bring in customers for feedback earlier in the process, FastWorks teams really did have the green light to fail, and fail faster, but on a smaller scale.[93]

The mindset of solving customer problems better and faster has gone so far as to lead GE to crowdsource answers to the world's toughest problems with both internal and external input. They believe that by *sourcing and supporting innovative ideas, wherever they might come from, and applying GE's scale and expertise, GE's approach to open innovation is helping to address customer needs more efficiently and effectively."* [94]

GE's Open Innovation Manifesto starts out by saying:

> *"We believe openness leads to inventiveness and usefulness... We also believe that it's impossible for any organization to have all the best ideas, and we strive to collaborate with experts and entrepreneurs everywhere who share our passion to solve some of the world's most pressing issues."* [95]

While GE has a significant leg up on its peers, it wasn't quick work to get to this point. It was, however, a constant focus on innovation that got them here. According to Linda Boff, executive director, global brand marketing:

"We've been around for 122 years and we're about invention, reinvention, and introducing new products—some of which have become their own industries. We see ourselves as being in perpetual motion. For example, we talk about how there are fireworks and campfires. You never let your campfire go out. At GE, those are constant research and development, innovation, leadership, globalization, simplification, and operating in a lean, fast manner. That's our foundation. The fireworks are bigger things that will pop out, and they will change because the market changes." [96]

Boff pointed out that 10 years ago, one of GE's fireworks was Ecomagination, the company's commitment to technology solutions that save money and reduce environmental impact:

"It started as a firework, and now it's how we do business. It's a campfire now." [97]

LIQUID LEARNING TRANSFORMS INTO LIQUID PROCESSES

As new types of team structures develop a history of working together and delivering success, marketers can show how our work will truly transform the business. And that ultimately demonstrates the value of the work we do as marketers.

To achieve this result, we must relentlessly pursue customer value by always thinking about the customer experience we're creating. Be an advocate for customers at all times and share these thoughts with others within the organization. While the push for change and innovation must be constant, that doesn't mean that change comes overnight. Boff pointed out that GE has had the same relentless focus for the last decade:

"The big themes that [CEO] Jeff [Immelt] talks about today are the same from 10 years ago—globalization, leadership, invention, and so forth. We believe that what we do is about making the world a better place. But the transformation that has come about in the GE portfolio since 2005 has given us a cohesive story.

"We're all living in a world where the totality of how you experience the brand is important. It's about how you show up. The world is so transparent and people are able to talk about their experiences first hand."[98]

Putting yourself in a challenging environment is one thing, but being able to cope with the pressure of that challenge is another. It's important to be able to handle the stress that comes with the unfamiliar situations that creating and implementing new frameworks within your organization will create. It's unrealistic to take all that we've covered in this book and expect it to be implemented in a matter of months. Change within organizations doesn't happen that quickly.

But if we aren't willing to start someplace and begin to experiment, we risk being left behind. New ideas, new platforms, and new media all matter. It's not about grabbing the ship with both hands and trying as hard as we can to turn it. It's about placing little bets and learning. It's about trying little experiments and seeing what happens.

As marketers, our ability to continually learn and adapt will be what determines how well we'll be able to thrive in today's fluidly evolving environment.

ENDNOTES

88 Edelman, David and Heller, Jason. *Marketing Disruption: Five Blind Spots on the Road to Marketing's Potential.* McKinsey & Company, October 2014.

89 Mitchinson, Adam and Morris, Robert. *Learning About Learning Agility*, Center for Creative Leadership and Teachers College, Columbia University, April 2012.

90 http://venturebeat.com/2013/10/28/apples-170-billion-2013-amazing-and-amazingly-forgettable/ accessed November 7, 2014.

91 https://www.apple.com/pr/products/ipodhistory/ accessed November 7, 2014.

92 Ries, Eric. *The Lean Startup.* Crown Business, 2011.

93 http://www.businessweek.com/printer/articles/218259-general-electric-wants-to-act-like-a-startup Accessed November 7, 2014.

94 http://www.ge.com/about-us/openinnovation Accessed November 7, 2014.

95 http://www.ge.com/about-us/openinnovation Accessed November 7, 2014.

96 Interview with Carla Johnson, December 16, 2014.

97 Ibid.

98 Ibid.

afterword:
THE ANSWER TO "WHAT DO YOU *REALLY* DO?"

In Stephen Greenblatt's Pulitzer Prize-winning book, *The Swerve*, he tells the story of Poggio Bracciolini—who was trained as a "scriptor"—and how he ostensibly transformed the entire world.

In the pre-Renaissance world of early 1400s Rome, Poggio would be the equivalent of today's content strategist. His job as scriptor was to write the official documents. He was skilled enough at it that he rose through the ranks to become the secretary to Pope John XXIII. Poggio's passion, however, was "book hunting." He, like others, would travel throughout Europe and look (usually in monasteries) for ancient texts from authors of ancient Rome. The right book (or content) could propel a scriptor like Poggio to great fame.

The competition for this content was thick; the monasteries where many of these books were stored were hip to the agendas of these book hunters. Some of the more unscrupulous book hunters would try to steal the books, while others tried to buy them. In short, it took a fine combination of diligence, charm, and politics to come away with a great find.

While on one of his hunts in 1417, Poggio found himself in a monastic library in southern Germany. There, he found a copy of the ancient book/poem *On the Nature of Things* by the Roman poet and philosopher Lucretius. This book had disappeared for more than 1,000 years and the fact that it had survived was remarkable.

There are a number of extraordinary topics covered in *On the Nature of Things*, including the nature of man, the idea of free will, and evolution. But perhaps foremost is the idea that everything that one can know is made up of extraordinarily small particles, which was ostensibly an extension of the Greek Atomists.

In *The Swerve*, Greenblatt argues that it is Poggio's rediscovery of *On The Nature of Things,* and the ideas it represented, that "*swerved*" the direction of the world into the Renaissance.

Poggio could just as easily have accepted his job as a simple "scriptor" and created content for the organization he worked for. But, his passion and diligence for content led him to something that would ultimately spawn a renaissance.

We were very lucky to have our friend Eduardo Conrado, senior vice president – chief innovation officer of Motorola Solutions, write the foreword of this book. When we asked him to write it, the reasons were more than his stature in the industry. He truly represents the type of change agent that is driving the "renaissance in marketing" that he describes.

Our point: You never know when a diligence and passion for undiscovered content-driven experiences will result in something that might just change the world.

It is with this idea that we send you forward from this book into your own grand adventure. We invite you to remember something that Robert Rose's grandfather used to say to him:

> *"Every experience you create is the opportunity to have impact on someone. You choose—as well as get to experience yourself—what that impact will be."*

Our hope is that your answer to what you *really* do is:

> *"I create remarkable experiences."*

case studies:
FOUR STORIES TO INSPIRE YOUR TRANSFORMATION

AON LEVELS THE PLAYING FIELD

For Aon, trying to earn brand recognition and get out of the transactional rut was like shoveling quicksand. That is, until they partnered with Manchester United.

Content marketing has played a critical role within Aon for the last 15 years and serves as the core of how they create and deliver value to their customers. It's also core to the eight-year, $240 million sponsorship of Manchester United, which Aon signed in April 2013. *"Without content marketing, we can't explain what we do,"* Phil Clement, chief marketing officer for Aon, told *AdAge* in an interview about the partnership.[99] This sponsorship extended the relationship that Aon started in 2009 when it invested $130 million over four years to display the brand on Manchester United jerseys.

That's not the only part of the relationship. Aon delivers solutions for United in 20-plus areas and played a key role in Manchester United's initial public offering (IPO), providing advice on the best strategies and options for access to capital. Aon Benfield helped raise $233 million for Manchester United's IPO and was a co-manager in syndicating the equity necessary to complete the transaction. As a result, discussing the work Aon does for Manchester United provides a noteworthy and memorable way to explain what Aon does.

Evolving the Industry

Aon serves as an intermediary between insurance companies and buyers so that buyers can make smarter decisions. For example, if a company is building a major facility overseas, they need someone to advise them on the project and broker the insurance to give investors the confidence to green light the effort. But there's so much to know about these wildly complex projects that whether or not a client is able to move forward often depends on the content they can find that will help them make decisions.

"For us, early on we hired thought leaders," Clement said. *"It was an investment because we were looking at the problems we wanted to solve for our customers, not just looking at transactions in insurance."*

"Thought leaders" meant professionals—some with Ph.D.s—in data, analytics, multi-variant regression, engineering fusion, and economics who could model the flow of capital as it moves around the world. *"We looked at how all of this went into the cost of a solution,"* he explained. *"You have to account for your investments in a different way. Investment is where a lot of companies lose their fortitude and one day they find out that they're in a place where they'll become extinct."*

That's where Aon saw an incredible opportunity and has shifted their focus from transactions to consulting in order to add value. After working in this direction since 2000, the company has reached an interesting point. Every year there is less concentration of revenue coming from transactions and more from consulting fees. Making that shift, however, hasn't come quickly.

"We're halfway through the shift that started 15 years ago," Clement explained. *"And it will take another 15 years to conclude to a point where everyone isn't in a transaction industry but rather an information industry. It's hard; it requires a different kind of employee; our footprint looks different and what clients expect over time changes. But if an industry is moving forward aggressively and a company doesn't keep pace, a transaction becomes a commodity."*

Comprising 495 companies that have been put together by acquisition, the individual business units within Aon have created content and overseen its distribution. But now, as the company has higher expectations and goals for the brand and the section, they are consolidating activities so they can more actively manage the control of editorial calendars in every part of the globe.

One of the things that Clement's team has done to help people understand Aon's business is create an online hub that explains how the six services that it provides——capital, data and analytics, health, retirement, risk, and talent—benefit Manchester United. The company gives advice on expensive risks that companies face, such as compensation, pension, and how to keep employees healthy. Aon also offers counsel on how to lessen the impact of those risks and how to help employees. All of this is different from the risk-management industry from which Aon came.

Not Your Everyday Play

In struggling for brand recognition, Aon realized they needed a big partner to help with global recognition.

"We have 78,000 employees all over the world, but it's hard to find more than 3,000 people in one place. We needed something that we could rally around internally and also engage clients in the conversations that we needed to have. But first they needed to know who we were."

Clement got approval from his executive team by showing how the sponsorship supported the company's goals. *"When you show up with an idea that focuses on things that the C-suite wants to accomplish, it's easier. We had strategic uniformity between the Manchester United sponsorship and what we wanted to accomplish for the company."* The things he hoped to accomplish included:

- **Brand awareness.** The Manchester United sponsorship gave Aon an explosion of brand awareness. This proved particularly true in developing markets that are important for the company, such as Korea and Brazil. Once the market knew that Aon existed, it also made it easier to answer the question: What, exactly, does Aon do?

- **Creating a common conversation.** Aon used their sponsorship of Manchester United to get people to engage in the spirit of the company in ways that would have been difficult without it.

They were able to catalyze the energy of the company and the sport in many ways, one of which was to take three balls from a game in Manchester and fly them to southern-most points in the world where Aon had offices—the tip of South America, the tip of South Africa, and the southern side of Australia. The balls were passed from employee to employee all the way back to London. As the balls arrived in offices, employees created content about the journey and talked about how Aon was impacting communities. It was engaging for clients to track and brought employees together with a common challenge.

- **Direct client engagement.** The six areas Aon operates in tie directly to the Manchester United team: capital, data and analytics, health, retirement, risk, and talent; this made it easy to tell the Aon story using Manchester United as an example. *"As companies, we know that access to capital is a big part of performing. A big part of Manchester United's strategy is how access to capital plays out on the field. For Aon to be able to tell that story through football is much more interesting."*

> "When you show up with an idea that focuses on things that the C-suite wants to accomplish, it's easier. We had strategic uniformity between the Manchester United sponsorship and what we wanted to accomplish for the company." | Phil Clement, Chief Marketing Officer, Aon

As important as this high-profile partnership has been for Aon, it has proven equally important for Manchester United in their efforts to raise capital. United's attractiveness to commercial partners stems from its unparalleled ability to reach global audiences. Its supporter base, alongside its rich history and tradition, makes the company uniquely appealing to sponsors. United, in turn, has been able to help Aon connect and engage with supporters; the club's relationship with Aon is key to this process.

Aon's sponsorship of Manchester United has brought Aon significant brand awareness and given the brand an interesting, almost universally relatable way to explain what it is that the company does.
Credit: Aon/Manchester United

"Partnerships such as the one with Aon clearly demonstrate how Manchester United provides a powerful global platform that enables our partners to amplify their brand and grow their business," said Richard Arnold, group managing director for Manchester United.

"Solid risk management advice and human capital solutions provided by Aon frees up capital for us to invest. As a result, our commercial segment has been growing at very fast rates, is highly profitable, and the revenue stream is highly predictable due to the long-term nature of our contracts. We

remain convinced that there are huge commercial opportunities out there for Manchester United, both in terms of categories as well as countries, and we are excited about the growth opportunity that lies ahead."

Redefining Value

Clement notes that the difficulties of content marketing are really underestimated.

"Any marketing organization that decides to move in this direction needs to focus first and foremost on understanding how they're creating value. Content strategies don't work when it's, 'We have a solution, now write about it.' It has to be at the core of the value creation process. It's important as a marketer and an enterprise to understand how you're perceived, the strategic value that you add, and if you're creating value for your company and your industry."

Success also depends on the talent of the team. Clement is still working on this. In order to create great, compelling content, a company has to have people with varied skills—not just B2B writing, but writing for television, magazines, and anywhere content needs to live. *"We look for people who've been in places where content is important,"* he said, *"places where they live and die by the quality rather than just writing to a project plan."*

In It to Win It

Does fortitude pay off? It certainly has for Aon. They've gone from an unknown, second-place runner to a well-known number one in their industry. When it comes to dollars, that translates into almost doubling revenue from $6 billion to $11 billion and market cap from $13 billion to $28 billion.

"We're in a completely different category of how the market perceives our brand than before," Clement pointed out. *"Where before we were in relative obscurity and firmly planted in second place in the heads of many clients, we're now recognized by more people on the planet than not, and recognized as the most credible in our space by people who make those decisions."*

ENDNOTES

99   http://adage.com/article/btob/content-marketing-plays-role-aon-manchester-united-deal/294282/

100 http://www.businessweek.com/articles/2013-12-05/the-rise-and-fall-of-blackberry-an-oral-history

BLACKBERRY IS BACK IN BLACK

When BlackBerry came out with the device of the same name in 1999, it turned the mobile industry upside down. The company forever changed customer expectations of the work environment by creating the true definition of "mobility." The 15-year-old Canadian company was known by few until it released BlackBerry, which made it easy, secure, and effective for people to send and receive emails while they were away from their desk.

In the beginning, the company focused on business customers; one of its earliest fans was Michael Dell. In the decade after it released BlackBerry, the company grew to become one of the world's most valuable tech companies, and both business and consumers lined up in droves to get the latest device. Oprah Winfrey named it one of her "favorite things" in 2003, exploding brand awareness. In 2006, BlackBerry came out with the Pearl, which had a camera and could play video; this entrenched it in the consumer market. The employee base went from approximately 2,000 employees to 12,000. One chief technology officer described the allure of BlackBerry as "digital heroin."[100]

From CrackBerry to ShrinkBerry

In 2007, the stock price was over $200 a share and in 2008 the company was valued at $83.4 billion, putting it shoulder to shoulder with companies like Goldman Sachs. In 2009, BlackBerry tallied approximately 15 million device sales each quarter. But employees began to see corporate CIOs carrying iPhones, a sure sign that the spunkier Apple phone was cannibalizing its corporate customer base. By third quarter 2013, BlackBerry device sales plummeted to 5 million per quarter.

BlackBerry was suffering from a lack of focus—consumer versus enterprise—and a chronic problem of overpromising and under delivering. Internally, employees weren't held accountable and deadlines came and went without consequences. Management focused on competition from sexier providers like Apple and Android and let their attention on the enterprise market wane.

Competitors and nimble startups cannibalized BlackBerry's position with existing customers during the bring-your-own-device movement. They also weren't talking directly to their enterprise customers. The market for devices had been changing dramatically and executives were too scattered and inattentive to lead employees through the necessary change.

In 2013, sales fell 56% and the company cut about 4,500 employees, or about 40% of their workforce. BlackBerry also began to seek a buyer to take the company private.

"Reports of our death are greatly exaggerated"

In December 2013, BlackBerry brought in a new CEO. John Chen was the former CEO of Sybase, where he righted the sinking company and turned it around to sell to SAP for $5.8 billion. One of his first actions was to send an open letter to customers and drive a stake in the ground about BlackBerry's future:

> *"We are very much alive, thank you."*

> *"Our 'for sale' sign has been taken down and we are here to stay."* [101]

Next came clear focus on their market: the enterprise customer. BlackBerry had an installed base of more than 80,000 customers that accounted for 80% of revenue.

Before BlackBerry could instill confidence in customers, they had to instill confidence in employees. That started by reiterating that BlackBerry was no longer for sale and had enough cash to survive beyond the next several quarters of expected losses.

Mark Wilson, senior vice president of marketing, said that instilling the brand story—making BlackBerry synonymous with work—took center stage. He wanted anyone looking for greater productivity, efficiency, security, and privacy to choose BlackBerry.[102] And it required employees to understand and believe it before they could get customers to do the same.

Wilson pointed out: *"Our vision is simple and clear and people understand where they fit in. You either make the company money or you save money. If you don't do one of these, then you will change. That sends a clear message for employees when it's delivered."*

In an article he published on LinkedIn, Chen discussed why employees were key to executing a turnaround in the right way. Here's how BlackBerry did just that:

- **Create a problem-solving culture.** When things go bad, everyone knows what went wrong, but few understand the way out. Focusing on the problems creates a negative environment and brings people down. BlackBerry continually reminded employees about finding solutions, not problems.

- **Maintain the sense of urgency.** Once you begin to make progress, it's easy to let up and catch your breath. BlackBerry made cutting costs and growing revenue clear to every employee at every turn.

- **Take care of your company like it's your home.** It's just as important to sweat the small stuff with a business you care about as it is with a family. Small things at scale add up to big impacts. For example, one manager had eight telephone accounts for employees who had already left but the company was still paying for them. Would you keep eight phones lines at your home if you only used one?

- **Know thyself.** The ancient Greeks had it right; truly know—and live—your focus. This helps employees make the small, daily decisions that keep you on course to your long-term goal.

- **Empower employees to take risks.** Many people know what's right; they're just afraid to say something. Let opportunities be a part of your culture.

- **Everyone has a role.** If you empower employees and it's okay to take risks, they'll speak up when they need to and solve problems earlier on. Everyone, at every level, can make a difference. Siloed organizations make it hard to share ideas. A turnaround culture lets everyone pitch in to get things done.[103]

It's one thing to say these six steps are how you change—and save—a company; it's another to actually execute on it. As a high-profile vendor with a huge social and blog audience (nearly 50 million social followers at the end of 2014 and 1 million blog readers a month), BlackBerry had a platform from which to tell their turnaround story. Brand journalism has become a key tactic. This has given them the ability to tell the story, externally, of how their device makes life easier for their enterprise customers. It's also central to tell the story of how the company delivers on the priorities set out by Chen—cutting costs and making money. As a proponent and practitioner of frugal marketing, Wilson knows that brand journalism doesn't require a lot of money but it does require proper execution and smart, consistent delivery.

"Many companies built their intranets in the late 1990s and haven't invested to keep them current as an internal publishing tool. Our intranet is absolutely a critical part of telling our story to employees; it's something that we take very seriously because it's THE communication channel for us to connect with our internal audience," Wilson pointed out. *"It's not marketing hype; they're interesting stories written from a journalism perspective."*

BlackBerry has one person who sources content from many places, writes, publishes, and operationalizes the process. The content is then tracked in terms of views, comments, and likes to see which stories are trending and what ideas reasonably engage the attention of employees. BlackBerry also uses tried-and-true email, town halls, and in-person meetings with employees and their supervisors that cascade from Chen's team to talk about what's going on in the company.

EMPLOYEE SPOTLIGHT: JAMES LEPP
Meet James Lepp who works in Ottawa as a Standards Manager.

Performance Reviews Assigned January 12
New training is available to help with your performance reviews.

Employee Spotlight: James Lepp
Meet James Lepp, who works in Ottawa as a Standards Manager.

BES12 Internal Rollout Now Complete
Great new highlights from the recent BES12 internal rollout.

Internet of Things Platform Unveiled
BlackBerry's IoT platform leverages our extensive technology portfolio.

JANUARY 07, 2015 • 12:15PM EST

BlackBerry Software on NantHealth HBox

New mobile HBox device captures and transmits vital medical information.

15 | 1 | 827

JANUARY 07, 2015 • 12:15PM EST

BBM Support for Wearable Technology

BBM will be available on a wide range of Android Wear smartwatches.

8 | 7 | 919

DECEMBER 10, 2014 • 12:20PM EST

Join the BBM Meetings Beta

We need more people trying BBM Meetings. It's easy — find out how.

4 | 14 | 1,056

JANUARY 07, 2015 • 12:00PM EST

AT&T to Carry BlackBerry Classic and Redesigned BlackBerry Passport

Both devices will be available in the near future.

17 | 13 | 1,253

JANUARY 07, 2015 • 11:00AM EST

Darkhotel APT Targeting Executives

A new cyber threat targets business executives travelling to high-end hotels.

3 | 5 | 1,283

JANUARY 05, 2015 • 4:00PM EST

BlackBerry QNX Announcements at CES

BlackBerry QNX is now in 50 million vehicles - a new milestone in the automotive market.

34 | 14 | 1,909

JANUARY 05, 2015 • 9:00PM EST

BlackBerry Passport Named 'Most Innovative Smartphone'

Find out why 91mobiles named the BlackBerry Passport the "Most Innovative Smartphone of the Year".

27 | 0 | 778

DECEMBER 24, 2014 • 9:00AM EST

BlackBerry Square: A Year in Review

We take a look back at the biggest stories of the year.

13 | 4 | 1,570

DECEMBER 24, 2014 • 8:30AM EST

Catching Up on Enterprise Offerings

Inside BlackBerry for Business summarizes some Enterprise announcements.

1 | 2 | 1,071

DECEMBER 23, 2014 • 12:00PM EST

Enhancements to Salesforce.com

Learn about the exciting changes happening in Salesforce this January.

4 | 0 | 829

DECEMBER 23, 2014 • 11:30AM EST

Updates to the BlackBerry EPP Program

EPP will be moving to an online-only model.

7 | 43 | 2,966

DECEMBER 23, 2014 • 10:30AM EST

Proud2Be: Spreading Cheer – Winners Announced!

Find out who won this year.

16 | 11 | 890

BlackBerry relies on its intranet, BlackBerry Square, as the core of its hub for making its brand story real and consistent for employees. Credit: BlackBerry

"Content marketing is as critical to employees as it is to customers," Wilson said. *"Just as you're trying to drive engagement with your target external audience, you have to do the same thing with employees. They're part of the conversation at all times, particularly in a turnaround. BlackBerry Square is our publication hub, and it looks, feels, and acts like a news site."*

> "If people don't consistently hear a focus on the strategy of the company, they focus on activities instead of outcomes."
> | Mark Wilson, SVP Marketing, BlackBerry

Employees interact and contribute to conversations through BlackBerry Square, even by simply "liking" an article. Wilson also measures engagement through the employee's journey, similar to how the brand measures engagement through the customer's journey.

"Similar to a customer's journey with a brand, companies need to drive awareness, engagement, and conversion of the company's strategy with employees to ensure they viscerally understand it and how it benefits customers," Wilson continued.

"Just as it's critical to deliver on each step of the customer journey, it is similarly critical to deliver on each step of the employee journey. Once this is in place, teams can focus on delivering outcomes that support the strategy rather than performing a set of activities that may be disconnected from the strategy. You have to keep pounding the awareness and engagement of the message and bake it into the culture."

A Shift in Perspective

Shifting perspective back to the enterprise customer has meant that BlackBerry had to evaluate what they looked for in candidates when recruiting, particularly for the sales team. *"We had to tell the business-to-business story through our recruiting process so we could find people who already understood what customers wanted and how to serve them,"* Wilson explained.

This proved especially true with the enterprise sales teams. BlackBerry had to help them learn to tell a different story that wasn't about QWERTY keyboards and battery life. Instead, they talked about massive hybrid connectivity at the enterprise level and how people expect to work in a mobile-first environment. This makes security and privacy that much more important. From the enterprise sales teams to carriers, BlackBerry focused on teaching this audience to solve business problems for their customers and avoid leading with tech specs.

Back that up one step further and you're at research and development. Ensuring that these teams understand the brand story and the urgency of delivering it through a product experience means broader and deeper collaboration between groups. Researching around the enterprise customer and delighting them on their terms affected industrial design and the user experience of device software.

Making BlackBerry Synonymous With Work

The key to the success of BlackBerry's quick turnaround, Wilson said, has been their ability to define a strategy and communicate it effectively and consistently to many audiences. To do that, the company clearly defined its story (making BlackBerry synonymous with work), told it with rigorous consistency, and worked to operationalize it in ways that drove growth and streamlined costs. Harnessing the collective influence of employees has given BlackBerry the ability to amplify the story through more people, making the new BlackBerry experience come alive for external audiences.

One year into the job of turning BlackBerry around, the company is now on firmer financial footing, posting its first profitable quarter in years, and looking for opportunities to grow by delivering the communications, collaboration, security, and privacy required by mobile professionals.

ENDNOTES

101 http://bizblog.blackberry.com/2013/12/john-chen-open-letter/

102 http://adage.com/article/btob/blackberry-marketing-chief-mark-wilson-talks-challenges/294139/

103 https://www.linkedin.com/pulse/20141027115155-14119785-the-keys-to-executing-a-turnaround-the-right-way

EMERSON BRINGS SEXY BACK

As a 125-year old, $24 billion global manufacturing company with 133,000 employees heavily rooted in an engineering heritage, Emerson's marketing team had historically struggled for attention and credibility.

Since Kathy Button Bell became chief marketing officer for Emerson in 1999, however, she has reengineered both the company's leadership role as well as marketing's role within the organization. She kicked off her stint with a massive rebranding effort that dropped the "Electric" part of the company's name and brought 35 autonomous sub-brands under one umbrella. Then she got down to business.

A Well-Engineered Story

Button Bell and her team have cultivated a brand story that resonates with businesses around the world and infiltrates every niche of the brand— from research and development to human resources and new business models. Emerson's "Consider It Solved" story centers on reducing complexity and how the company solves people's problems. Every story the company tells and every activity they take part in stems from the "Consider It Solved" story.

"In the beginning, we realized we weren't telling meaningful, problem-solving stories," Button Bell said. *"Back then, we told stories just about our products, but didn't have a dialogue. Now, because of social media, we have 133,000 employees trying to tell stories and create a dialogue. We figured out how to*

aggregate it and keep it in sync so we didn't appear insane as a company. It had to feel like there's a main story."

Instilling a culture of storytelling doesn't come quickly in any company. For an engineer-led brand like Emerson, it's even harder—but doable.

A key for Emerson's success has been bringing the story to life internally first. By putting the "Consider It Solved" mantra front and center, Button Bell's team has created an emotional connection with employees. Through color, light, and sound, she's refreshed the perception of the brand, transforming it from an old, staid company to one that feels young, bright, and bold.

It's Never Been Done Before

Button Bell brought a litany of firsts to the table. Drawing both on her background in consumer marketing research and the zealous curiosity of her boss, Charlie Peters, she embedded market research as core to the marketing team. From that research data, she focused attention on two vital areas.

First: Marketing needed to move "upstream" and champion the voice of the customer by becoming intimately involved in research and development from the beginning. Emerson calls this "Stage Gate Zero."

"We launched products and had disappointing results," Button Bell explained. *"We saw that the research upfront didn't ask customers what they wanted. Engineers ask feature-oriented questions, which don't get to real innovation. Good market-research people get to benefits and what problems the customer wants to solve."*

Second: Doubling down on market research meant that the Emerson marketing team had a better sense of where to reach their audience. In addition to tried-and-true trade publications, Button Bell expanded into TV (Fox News, the Golf Channel, CNN International, BBC, and domestic and international cable channels) as well as mainstream print media, digital, and airport advertising, all of which were unheard of for a traditional B2B brand.

"We learned that our core audience was comprised of decision makers at global Fortune 1000 companies," Button Bell said. *"These were the top executives in the world. We're more likely to catch executives watching these channels as they travel around the world than we are while they're in their own homes."*

Marketing Moves Mainstream

In recent years, the biggest trend has been to elevate the role of marketing within Emerson so that people acknowledge and recognize its importance. To set aside apprehension and to build engagement with others outside of marketing, Button Bell has excellent examples of what has worked well. One example is The Extra Mile blog from Charlie Peters, Emerson's senior executive vice president (TheExtraMileWithCharlie.com). The blog has a central strategy that tells a consistent story over time. Peters' online presence took into consideration the cadence of his tweeting to drive traffic to his blog, which has realized great success. Peters' efforts reflect well on Emerson and educate people internally about opportunities.

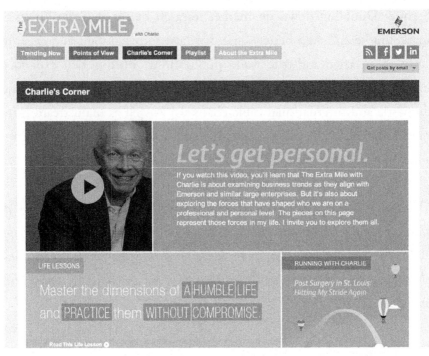

Emerson uses the success of Senior Vice President Charlie Peters' blog to build engagement with others within the company and show the success of content efforts. Credit: Emerson

"We've taken an extremely senior executive and turned him into a communications vehicle," Button Bell said. *"We've allowed him to be personal. Charlie's an expert on business, but he's also a runner and an expert on that, too. He shares letters to his son in Afghanistan. Life lessons from a different decade. It's interesting and poignant, not just the normal business topics. You can't fake Charlie's level of authenticity."*

Button Bell also looked for ways to break down silos and mesh functions whenever possible in order to keep the voice of the customer front and center. Turning toward things that aren't traditional marketing responsibilities, like integrating the internal and external message and experience, has been a big reason why Emerson has been able to drive a successful, cohesive customer experience.

Button Bell's team has redefined the different flavors of roles that marketers need in order to inspire employees and build collaboration across the enterprise. Drawing on career resource information from the University of Michigan about the traits that make a successful marketer, Button Bell went beyond looking at functional roles, and instead focused on the bigger picture. She outlined the functions as:

Project Manager: Role–execution. Project managers not only run programs and manage campaigns, they oversee IT projects. They also implement the recruiting messaging for human resources, so the company brings the right talent into the organization. This role makes sure that marketing collaborates with other functions within the company.

Analyst: Role–analyze. This team member is in charge of assembling and mining databases for relevant information. He or she also manages quantitative research.

Artist: Role–communicate. As a communicator, this marketer "architects" the brand and oversees how it's being expressed. He or she sculpts the image and perception of Emerson, and articulates the range of knowledge that its experts share.

Psychologist: Role–feel. By smashing the traditional engineering perspective of a highly rational-based approach to customers, the psychologist understands qualitative market research. He or she then develops personas and explores customer perceptions of Emerson's brand and product.

Orchestrator
Advocates customer experience
Drives relationship/reputation
Connects to other functions/integrator-internal audiences

Lead

Psychologist
Understands market research (qualitative)
Develops personas
Explores customer perceptions

Feel

Artist
Architects brand
Sculpts image
Articulates knowledge

Communicate

Analyst
Assembles and mines databases
Manages quantitative research

Analyze

Project Manager
Runs programs
Oversees IT projects
Manages campaigns
Implements recruiting messaging
Collaborates with other functions

Execute

Emerson has defined the different roles they need marketing to fulfill in order to connect with customers, understand research, articulate learnings, collaborate with other groups, and then manage and execute the work. Credit: Emerson

Orchestrator: Role–lead. As an orchestrator, this marketer keeps things humming so all the parts and pieces are choreographed to get things done. He or she advocates for the customer experience. By connecting to other functions and integrating with internal audiences, the orchestrator also drives relationships and the reputation of marketing within the organization.

"Business-to-business companies, especially the more you get into manufacturing and heavy industrial companies, value the project manager and analyst," Button Bell pointed out. *"Those are things that engineers can get their head around. Some may see the point of an artist, but not necessarily value it. But when it comes to the psychologist and orchestrator, that's where marketers bring incredible value, but you can't measure it in a traditional engineering way. Marketing teams need this blend of flavors in order to evangelize the customer and create a seamless, intuitive business experience. That's incredibly hard, but critical, especially in complex, siloed B2B companies like Emerson."*

The Empowered Employee

Coming back full circle to where Button Bell started—with employees—in order to empower and elevate marketing, she needed to expand the idea of the empowered customer to that of the empowered employee.

"We've all acknowledged the empowered customer, but it's time to recognize the empowered employee," Button Bell asserted. *"The digital age has brought exceptional transparency and honest views to all employees. We need that for a company the size and scale of Emerson. In order to successfully drive cohesion and a seamless customer experience, we have to communicate as aggressively and consistently internally as we do externally."*

There's no group within the enterprise more suited to take on this task because marketers are natural communicators. Button Bell's team is taking its skill in mapping customer journeys to create an employee journey. This will help the company understand what matters to potential high-performing employees, how to find them and capture their attention, how to woo them into an employment relationship, and how to nurture, grow, and retain them as valuable leaders at all levels of the organization.

Marketing has the talent to help human resources narrowly target an employee audience—just like it does a customer audience——and bring the Emerson brand alive by creating passionate, emotional connections.

"The experience generation is coming up behind us, and we will need to create incredibly customizable and personal experiences," Button Bell said. *"As marketers, we give customers as well as employees something to aspire to."*

MOTOROLA SOLUTIONS FINDS PURPOSE THROUGH CHAOS

For the last five years, Motorola Solutions has been on a trajectory that has led them through a company split, a complete rebranding, redefining the role of the CMO, and essentially upending the purpose of marketing within the company. And they're not done yet.

In the Beginning

In January 2011, Motorola, Inc. spun off its consumer-focused division and became two separate companies: B2B-focused Motorola Solutions and Motorola Mobility, which Google bought in 2012 and Lenovo acquired in October 2014.

As the senior vice president - chief innovation officer for Motorola Solutions, Eduardo Conrado posed the question: How do you create an 80-year-old startup?

"We had lost the attention of the marketplace over the previous 20 years," Conrado said. *"But with a 'new' company, we had the opportunity to refocus and recapture that attention. We went through extensive exercises related to brand purpose that defined the company's promise, voice, and values. We're the people who guide you through the higher-level solutions, and we wanted to be seen as trusted advisers. So whether Motorola Solutions sells the product or not, how can we solve problems for our customers?"*

The company split was an inflection point that began a transformative journey for Motorola Solutions to shift the market's perception of them from a provider of products to a trusted adviser of solutions.

Creating a Purpose-Driven Brand

In preparation for the split, Conrado's first step was to redefine the company through a story that articulated the brand purpose. More than 80 years ago, Motorola began with the invention of the car radio and later, car radios for police. In fact, the company name was formed by linking "motor" (for motorcar) with "ola" (which implies sound). Thus, the Motorola brand meant sound in motion. Through the decades, Motorola evolved into delivering communication products to vertical markets such as retail, government, and public safety.

Conrado's team tied the history of the company into their purpose as a brand focused on their core roots and the impact they would have on customers. In lieu of focusing on products, Motorola Solutions articulated their brand purpose: helping people be their best in the moments that matter.

The marketing team spent a year instilling the brand purpose internally within the company and expanded its influence on the culture by collaborating heavily with human resources.

"Our internal values and external promise tied back to the brand purpose," Conrado explained. *"We didn't want our values to be just a poster on the wall; we wanted to make sure that they genuinely resonated with employees."*

Conrado's team used the brand purpose as the foundation that led into leadership behaviors and storytelling that inspired employees. This built deep engagement for employees and explained how the company was transitioning from talking about the products they sell to discussing the meaningful difference they deliver. For example, instead of talking about the technical specifications of the handsets they sell to police officers, they told the story of what they enable an officer to do—save lives.

Architecting Systems of Engagement

While going through the discovery of their brand purpose, Motorola Solutions also looked at how to streamline, bring consistency to, and scale their content creation and management system. They had always done well with their strategy and execution relating to thought leadership. However, they realized that they needed to improve both sales enablement and demand generation. A big question the Motorola Solutions team faced was: With hundreds of people publishing globally, how do we ensure they work in concert with a unified corporate story, avoid duplicate efforts, and yet preserve the individuality of regions and vertical markets?

"We have key verticals and each breaks into three pillars for our content strategy—thought leadership, demand generation, and sales enablement," Conrado said. *"We spent a great deal of time talking to marketing and sales so they understood the approach, and so we could understand the nuances of maintaining that individuality for regions and vertical markets. When it comes to the technology that supports this process, our focus isn't on cost savings, it's on better alignment of our efforts and creating systems of engagement for our customers."*

With the company split, each function within the organization sought to rid itself of legacy overhead by:

- Eliminating anything that didn't add value to customer relationships

- Stimulating imagination and innovation with employees

- Differentiating investments, focus, and partnerships toward specific customer segments

- Looking to the future to move Motorola Solutions' purpose—helping people be their best in the moments that matter—forward faster.

To do this, Conrado identified four key mindsets:

- **Engagement.** Evolve selling and marketing processes and organizational structures from Products (1.0), to Solutions (2.0), to Trusted Advisers (3.0).

- **Innovation.** Innovation would transition from the domain solely of a dedicated engineering and design group into the responsibility of all employees.

- **Operations.** While excellent, the company's operational processes were less relevant to driving business growth. Motorola Solutions kept processes core to customer delivery and then looked at how to transform, simplify, and optimize them.

- **Reskilling.** The company's focus on the talent of its people moved from specific transactions to that of attracting and growing new talent and skills in specialties that differentiated the company.

The evolution of the purpose of the IT organization within Motorola Solutions reflected the changing view that the company had of its customers: from products to solutions, from order-taker to adviser, from transactional to lifecycle.

Creating the MIT Ecosystem

Prior to the spin-off of Motorola Mobility, Motorola's marketing team set the objectives and priorities for technology within the group and had a dotted line partnership with IT. As the company split and Conrado focused on integrating marketing technologists into the mix, the roles of marketing and IT have ebbed and flowed over the years. *"It's never been a situation where marketing submits a business case to IT and the IT team goes off and manages the RFPs,"* Conrado pointed out. *"It has always been a team that works together jointly and to the point where it has been hard to distinguish if someone worked in marketing or IT. And that really told us something: maybe there's a more efficient way to manage the process."*

In January 2013, Motorola Solutions' CIO began reporting to Conrado, thus creating an efficient, single structure. This move into a hybrid environment better enabled the marketing team to architect solutions, select vendors, and build systems for both front-office and back-office interactions.

The decision to blend marketing and IT into one group (MIT) was aided by research from Gartner. In it, analysts highlighted that just over one-third of CIOs report directly to a CEO. That means two-thirds report through another function. If it's under operations, the CIO's focus will be on supply chain and distribution channels. Under the CFO, it will be costs. But under the CMO, the CIO will focus on systems of engagement (i.e., anything that interacts with a customer, from a single portal for channel partners to systems for direct sales) and the customer while providing a holistic view on how the IT function can be a strategic differentiator for the company.

"That's the emphasis we wanted for technology," Conrado said, *"to have an IT staff that worked with marketing to hone in on customers to create systems of engagement."*

"That's the emphasis we wanted for technology...to have an IT staff that worked with marketing to hone in on customers to create systems of engagement." | Eduardo Conrado, Senior Vice President - Chief Innovation Officer, Motorola Solutions

Marketing benefits from this in two ways. First, with 15,000 employees worldwide, the IT systems make it easier to identify internal experts and bring visibility to them both internally and externally. Second, marketing benefits from improved knowledge and content management. Motorola Solutions focuses a lot of its marketing and IT efforts on systems of engagement. Conrado views IT as a strategic differentiator and a potential revenue generator.

"We're a company that believes in integrating marketing and the systems of engagement with customers," Conrado said. *"This is why marketing and IT fall under one person. Technology is the enabler for the message developed by marketing to better reach our customers."*

Intelligently Creating Content

Building systems of engagement with customers was one challenge. Making sure that information could also be distributed internally and collaboratively to break down silos in the process proved to be quite another.

Because almost 70% of a customer's content consumption was digital, Motorola Solutions' marketing teams needed to evaluate the performance of content continually. Conrado wanted a technology ecosystem that could empower his team and provide content testing and personalization to better understand what generated action.

In late 2014, Conrado hired a new type of CIO. Instead of focusing on traditional back-office activities and keeping the lights on, this CIO is customer-centric and focused on driving engagement, growth, and innovation. He's developed a holistic view of the customer journey and focuses heavily on what marketing and sales need in terms of developing and maintaining the customer experience.

"Marketers must understand the need to be metrics-driven in order to survive and thrive," Conrado elaborated. *"The only way to justify what you do and be considered the indispensable partner of sales and finance is to have the right tools at your disposal. If you're a company and still have the mentality of 'if you build it, they will come,' then IT doesn't have a role in your space. At Motorola Solutions, we're metrics-driven marketers; we can't do our jobs properly without the upfront investment. Unless you understand where the prospect is, where they've been, and how they've been engaged, you're shooting in the dark. Without integrating IT into marketing, you'll always remain at the segment of mass audience and mass message. In 10 years, marketing will be radically more metrics-based, so IT has to become your hand-in-hand partner today."*

Opportunity Keeps Knocking

In early 2014, the company announced that it would sell 40% of its assets to Zebra Technologies. This gave Conrado the opportunity to pull out a blank sheet of paper and "architect" the right systems of engagement from the ground up.

"Most companies don't have a big enough jolt to pause and take a long-range view of both marketing and technology that we've had," he explained. *"Many are still entrenched in the buy mode. But for Motorola Solutions, splitting the company in two, and then selling a portion a few years later gave us the opportunity to look at what the right technology stack was for us. We're able to move all of our systems worldwide to a platform that gives us greater simplification."*

Simplification also means the ability to better leverage content creators around the world. As the demand for targeted content increases, Motorola Solutions' technology now gives sales and marketing teams real-time visibility into what's being created, and then allows them to request and require input from others within the company. This has given every marketing person line-of-sight into what content is being created and, in most cases, makes it easy to localize for their specific market.

MSI SALES ENABLEMENT SYSTEMS STRATEGY

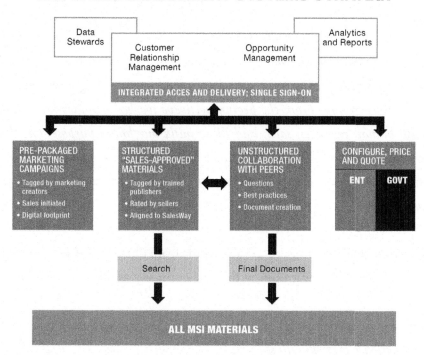

The ability for all marketers to have line-of-sight into content that's being created means that Motorola Solutions (MSI) has better consistency with its brand story, minimizes duplicate efforts, and creates better quality content to engage audiences. Credit: Motorola Solutions

"We had regions developing content around a solution or a vertical market, and other groups didn't know about it until they shared the final assets," Conrado continued. *"There was no line-of-sight into what was being developed. So we'd have duplicate content or we would see that we were going to market with two different points of view and we had to kill one. There was too much of a focus on content production and not enough on an engagement strategy."*

Concentrated Patience

What has Conrado and his team learned over the last five years?

"People get excited about what's possible. But the problem is that they don't have the human power, time, and money to do everything all at once. You have to take a building-block approach and that's why you need tight partnerships with other groups. From the beginning, we've worked shoulder-to-shoulder with human resources, sales, and IT to build our brand purpose and then engage audiences. With the point that we're at now, we need a technology architecture that will grow with us without over-engineering. That's a hard balance."

For Motorola Solutions, success has come from blurring the lines between marketing and other groups within the company as much as possible.

"It's a multi-year journey," Conrado said. *"You have to have the fortitude and patience to stick with it."*

acknowledgements:

Albert Einstein said, *"Life is like riding a bicycle. In order to keep your balance you must keep moving."*

We're very blessed to have an incredible group of friends who've kept us moving on the journey to bring this book to fruition. We'd like to thank them for their generosity, input, and guidance along the way.

First and foremost, to Joe Pulizzi, Pam Kozelka, and the entire CMI team for reopening their publishing doors. We have nothing but immense gratitude for the care and nurturing that we felt every step of the way.

For the overall structure and narrative, we want to thank Newt Barrett and his team of experts for their extraordinary efforts. He ensured that the story that was in our heads was translated, understandable, and ready to put into play for the rest of the world. Newt pushed us, and it shows in the finished work. For overall readability and accuracy, we want to profusely thank Lisa Murton Beets for her time and love. She is truly the Winston Wolfe of editing.

Credit for our beautiful cover design goes to the amazing and indefatigable Joseph Kalinowski. And we so appreciate the work of Diane Laney for the graphics and Yvonne Parks for layout. We also thank Eduardo Conrado for his eloquence in writing the foreword of this book and for continually keeping our eyes on the horizon of the profession we love so much.

There are many business leaders who helped us open the doors of this exploration. But, in particular, we'd like to thank those who helped make our experience of telling this story remarkable. They include: Carlos Abler, Thomas Asacker, Kathy Button Bell, Linda Boff, Phil Clement, Gurdeep Dhillon, Julie Fleischer, Tyler Gosnell, Steve Liguori, Antonio Lucio, Trevor Traina, and Mark Wilson. We are humbled by their talent and grateful for their generous nature.

For the thought leaders who have pushed our thinking and helped us pave this path, we want to acknowledge both their encouragement and valuable critique. If this book has merit, it's largely because of their input. They include Ardath Albee, Jay Baer, Michael Brenner, Andrew Davis, Lee Gallagher, Scott Liewehr, Cathy McKnight, Tim Washer, Dr. Tim Walters, and Todd Wheatland.

And last, we'd like to thank our families, especially our spouses, Elizabeth and Ron. We are incredibly blessed by loving, supportive, and delightfully interested families and we appreciate their eager support. You bring us the best experiences that life has to offer.

about the authors:

Robert Rose
Robert@contentinstitute.com
Twitter: @Robert_Rose
About.Me/RobertRose

Robert is chief strategy officer for the Content Marketing Institute and a senior contributing consultant for Digital Clarity Group.

His first book, coauthored with Joe Pulizzi, *Managing Content Marketing*, is widely considered the "owner's manual" for the content marketing process. It's been translated into multiple languages and spent several weeks as a top 10 marketing book on Amazon.com since its debut in 2011. Robert is also co-host of the podcast PNR's This Old Marketing, the #1 podcast as reviewed by MarketingPodcasts.com

As a recognized expert in content marketing strategy, digital media, and customer experience, Robert innovates creative and technical strategies for a wide variety of clientele. He has advised large enterprises such as 3M, Dell, AT&T, Federal Express, KPMG, Staples, PTC, and UPS. In addition, he has helped develop digital marketing efforts for entertainment and media brands such as Dwight Yoakam, Nickelodeon, and NBC.

An Internet pioneer, Robert has more than 20 years of experience and a track record of helping brands and businesses develop successful web and content marketing strategies. In the mid-1990s, Robert developed some of the first web strategies in the country for clients such as Mediamark Research (MRI), the Cable and Telecommunications Association (CTAM), and the U.S. government—literally introducing these leading organizations to the web.

Robert is a regular columnist for *EContent* and *Chief Content Officer* magazines, and a regular contributor for many others.

When he's not on an airplane somewhere around the world, Robert lives and loves in Los Angeles with his beautiful wife, Elizabeth, and their golden doodle, Daisy.

Carla Johnson
Carla@TypeACommunications.com
Twitter: @CarlaJohnson
About.Me/JohnsonCarla

Carla Johnson helps marketers unlock, nurture, and strengthen their storytelling muscle so they can create delightful experiences. Through her consultancy, Type A Communications, she works as a trusted adviser at the highest level of blue-chip brands to establish open conversations, instill creative confidence, and inspire an environment of receptivity that develops highly prized teams and stellar business value. Carla has worked with companies such as American Express, Dell, Emerson, Motorola Solutions, VMware, Western Union, and the U.S. Army Corps of Engineers on how to tap into a wellspring of ideas and unveil new ways to bring their brand stories to life in fun and captivating ways.

Recognized as one of the top 50 influencers in content marketing, Carla serves as vice president of thought leadership for the Business Marketing Association, a division of the Association of National Advertisers, and is an instructor for the Content Marketing Institute and the Online Marketing Institute. A frequent speaker, Carla also writes about the future of B2B marketing, leading through innovation, and the power of storytelling for the Content Marketing Institute, *Chief Content Officer* magazine, *CMSWire*, and other business and industry publications. Carla lives in Denver with her devilishly handsome husband, Ron, their three children, Melinda, Abby, and Nick, two parakeets, and seven fish.

CPSIA information can be obtained
at www.ICGtesting.com
Printed in the USA
LVOW05s0455030617
536792LV00001B/1/P